Helping Kids PERFORM

Mental Skills Every Parent, Teacher, and Coach Should Master!

Jacques Dallaire, Ph.D.

Dallaire Consulting LLC
Concord, NC

Published by
Dallaire Consulting LLC • Concord, NC

In cooperation with
The Book Couple • Boca Raton, FL
United Graphics and CreateSpace.com

www.HelpingKidsPerform.com
www.PerformancePrime.com

 www.facebook.com/PerformancePrime

@PerformPrime

ISBN: 978-0-9851461-2-2

Copyedited by Carol Rosenberg
Cover design by Vesperia, Inc.—Jay Welch
Book layout & design by Gary Rosenberg

Printed in the United States of America

A Note on Gender: The examples and discussions in this book can be applied to either gender. Therefore, the nonstandard "singular they" construction is used throughout this work to include both genders, as the English language has no singular pronoun for indeterminate gender.

This book is dedicated to all the parents, teachers, and coaches around the globe who want the best for the children who are entrusted into their care. Helping children to reach their full potential is a challenging job, and unfortunately, kids don't come with an instruction manual. As adults, we try to do the best we can, but sometimes we make mistakes. . . . I certainly know that I have. I wish I had known then what I know to be true now. Often, we don't really understand how the way we interact with our children affects how they think, how they feel, and ultimately, how they perform. In short, we don't know what we don't know, until we know it.*

I hope this book helps you to know it better.

---

* Please note that when I refer to your child or children going forward, I take it to mean the young people over whom you have influence, regardless of the role you play in that child's life (as a parent, teacher, coach, mentor, etc.).

Contents

Dr. Jacques's Rules of the Mental Road

Rule #1 If you want to climb out of a hole, the very first thing you must do is *stop digging!*

Rule #2 The mind can only actively process ONE thought *at a time.*

Rule #3 You can't *NOT* think about whatever is on your mind.

Rule #4 Your *dominant thought* determines your emotions, the behaviors that flow from those emotions, and ultimately, your ability to perform.

Rule #5 You *ARE in control* of your dominant thought.

Rule #6 Your *perception* or *perspective* regarding the challenges that you face will determine your dominant thought.

Rule #7 If you do what you've always done, you'll get what you've always gotten . . .
If you want something different, you must approach the challenges you face with a different mindset!

www.HelpingKidsPerform.com

Introduction

As a performance specialist, I've been in the fortunate position over the years to interact with and influence literally thousands of individuals involved in a broad variety of high-performance sports and high-risk/high-demand occupations. Many of my clients have been leaders in the business and occupational world, as well as champions in their respective competitive sports. I've learned much from these top professionals regarding the *real* world of high performance and the unique demands and challenges that exist in this world. My professional life has been dedicated to sharing with them insights and training strategies that they could then use to achieve and even exceed their personal performance goals.

But before you're mislead into thinking that this book is all about high-performance and, as a result, only relevant to individuals who operate at this level, let me assure you that nothing could be further from the truth. Over the years, it has become clear to me that many of the performance issues and problems that people operating at the highest levels wrestle with are *fundamentally the same* as those that everyone else wrestles with in their life. It's just that they may not encounter them quite as often as we do and the immediate consequences of not getting it right for them are sometimes more significant than they might be for us. The principles and tools that we'll discuss here are being used by some of the world's top performers, but they can also directly help you and members of your family improve your life and your personal performance as well.

While my background may be somewhat different from that of many "self-help" book authors in that I don't have a formal degree in psychology or psychiatry, besides my advanced degree in exercise physiology, I do have more than forty years of practical, real-world experience working with people in the high-performance domain. I have an army of very successful clients doing very different things all over the world who are utilizing the tools and relying on the principles that I will share with you in this book. Their collective experience reinforces the fact that these principles are fundamentally sound as well as universally applicable, and that the tools I will offer you are proven. I want you to have access to this information, which has been limited in the past to only the most high-level performers.

One of the key things that I've come to learn over the years is that no matter where my clients come from or what they do, they mentally sabotage themselves in much the same way. The underlying weakness that leads them all to this place is a common human trait that exists as a learned behavior—one that is often reinforced by people in their environment. We're not born with it, but we all insist on adopting it early on in our life. The underlying human trait that I'm referring to is our (seemingly) insatiable need to "worry." In the coming pages, I'll develop a framework to help you to understand where this comes from, how it impacts performance, and what you can do about it so that you're less likely to mentally sabotage yourself or have the same effect on your children. So what am I hoping to accomplish with this book?

My goal in writing this book is ultimately to help children of all ages become more successful within their chosen sport, as well as in life in general—hence the title *Helping Kids Perform*. But because children aren't likely to read this book or to necessarily understand the concepts that I discuss in its pages, I've targeted the book to parents, teachers, and coaches—those individuals who typically have the greatest impact on children and who *can* understand the concepts I put forward here.

As my reader, understand that you will be the immediate beneficiary of the material in this book. It's directed to you because it's as relevant to you as it is to any high-performance competitor . . . or to your child. It's important for you to apply these principles in your own life because, ultimately, your personal performance is important to the well-being of your child. It's also important for you to understand this material because, sometimes, you are unwittingly the agent of mental sabotage that your children must contend with and understanding things differently might just cause you to change your behavior. As parents or mentors, we don't intend to sabotage our children—it's just that we don't always realize the impact that the things we say and how we say them can affect our child's *mindset*.

You spend so much time focusing on the needs of your children, you can think of this as an opportunity to focus on your needs in a way that will help your children to benefit indirectly. As a friend described it, it's a little like the instructions we receive from the flight attendant who tells us that, in the advent of need, we should put on our own oxygen mask before we help those people around us with theirs.

Your children will benefit in the short term from your working through this book because when you've taken these principles to heart and integrated them into your life, you'll be less likely to contribute to their self-sabotage in the moments when they are called upon to perform. Longer term, your children will also benefit because your understanding and application of these principles in your own life will provide opportunities, by your example and through your instruction, for them to acquire this knowledge for themselves—in age-appropriate ways.

My goal is to help children indirectly through the adults who surround them to develop a set of *mental skills* that will serve them well as they seek to deliver their best performance in all that they do. It's also my hope that the mental skills they gradually develop will serve as a foundation for the way they think as they engage the many challenges that life will throw in their path. It's not just about performance though; it's about happiness and mental health as well.

I mentioned earlier that sometimes adults unwittingly become the agents of mental sabotage for the children they influence, and this is why I believe that this book is so necessary. Over the years, I've been exposed to many young competitors in a variety of situations where the adults in their environment helped to sabotage their performance. The very people who were supposed to support these young performers were the ones who unwittingly damaged the mindset that would have allowed them to be more successful. The interaction between adult and child visibly hurt the child's ability to deliver their best performance, and in some cases, it destroyed their desire to even continue to participate in the activity in question. As soon as they were of an age where they could make up their own mind about their participation, they decided they wanted nothing more to do with the sport or activity they were involved in. I've seen adults absolutely shatter a child's self-confidence and set them up for failure, in large measure because they imposed results-oriented expectations on them, many of which were completely unrealistic.

Unfortunately, this situation has proven to be all too common as well in the school environment, both in the classroom and on the playing field. It isn't because these adults didn't want their child to succeed. In fact, it's quite the opposite. It's just that they didn't understand *how* the way they sometimes interacted with these children negatively affected their mindset and, ultimately, their ability to perform.

I've also seen parents and coaches *knowingly* impose significant pressure on children because of a false belief that this would motivate the child to "try harder" and help them to become "mentally tough." There are plenty of examples of this kind of unfortunate thinking and behavior in the world of sport and beyond. As parents, how many of us have witnessed the appalling lack of self-control of some adults at the local baseball, ice hockey, soccer, or basketball game? Their hyper-competitiveness and insatiable need to win cause them to say and do things that not only shock other adults but also impact their children in significant ways. Their attempt to live vicariously through the exploits and successes of their children (because this may have always been a dream of theirs) is sometimes derailed and they become supremely frustrated, so they lash out when those dreams aren't realized. As role models for children, what are they teaching them by their example?

I don't intend to preach what I think is morally right or wrong, because children don't come with a "user manual," or at least, I certainly wasn't given one with mine. The choices we make as adults are always influenced by circumstances in the moment and by our own experiences, and who's to say that one choice is necessarily better than another. I will, however, share with you my observations—drawn from many years of practical experience—regarding how the things we say and the way we say them (both explicitly and implicitly) can affect a child's thinking and the mindset with which they approach the challenges that they undertake. I'll offer suggestions that have more to do with a *philosophy* of thinking that's been proven over the years to help people I've come to know get more out of themselves. This methodology of Performance Thinking has helped them to get out of their own way by reducing the extent to which they mentally sabotaged their own performance.

Competitiveness is a strong and indeed a natural force in the human species, and this is a good thing because it pushes us to work hard and continue to strive to overcome difficulties or obstacles that may lie in our path. The challenge is not to suppress this natural instinct but rather to teach children how to focus and channel it so that it's used at the right time (when the "game" is on) and at the proper intensity (not so strong that they forget about enjoyment and sportsmanship), and to turn it off when their competitiveness is inappropriate. It becomes a question of control. By teaching them how to manage and control their thinking, they can learn to optimize their personal performance rather than mentally sabotage it. And yet in my experience, the vast majority of people are quite adept at mentally sabotaging their own performance.

This book is *not* about the power of positive thinking, however. While positive thinking is better than negative thinking in terms of optimizing performance, thinking positively just isn't good enough by itself. We ourselves need to be *more* than just positive, and we need to help our children to do the same. Each of us knows people who are positive but who can't perform very well when the chips are down and it's "go" time. I've encountered such individuals throughout my career as a performance specialist. They are positive people who are happy and who see life's glass as being half full, but they don't perform particularly well on a consistent basis. Delivering our best performance isn't just about being happy with no process in place to help cement and sustain the mindset that's necessary to perform at our best.

What this book attempts to do is to help you to understand how your mind works as it relates to key basic mental skills and how these thought processes affect your ability to perform. It's also about the power and methodology of *dominant thought* and how positive and task-focused thinking allows you to gain control over your mind in a way that optimizes your personal performance, as opposed to sabotaging it.

I may not have all of the answers, but my experience in the high-performance world over the past forty years has provided me with a unique opportunity to study and understand how a lot of these pieces fit together. I won't suggest what activities your child should engage in because that's a personal choice, but I'll show you how you might help your child to maximize their performance in whatever that activity might be. I'll share with you a simple framework that I've created and used over the years as a "backbone" to help explain how this process of mental self-sabotage begins, how it evolves, and ultimately, how it affects your ability to perform. I call this framework the Rules of the Mental Road. These concepts and principles underpin a set of critical life skills that cut across all activities and all age groups. In my experience, this framework has proven to be:

- *Fundamental*—in that it derives from simple concepts related to the way the human mind processes information.
- *Universal*—in that it applies to everyone, regardless of culture, language, gender, age, or arena.
- *Infallible*—in that I have yet to find a single instance where the rules associated with this framework don't apply.

In Chapter 1, I'll discuss a fundamental concept that I believe underlies the single most common process by which we all mentally sabotage our own performance. This is true as much for your child as it is for you. I'm confident enough in the truth of this simple construct to state that when people get this right, they deliver their best performance, but when they don't, their performance is never as good as it might have been. This holds true for anyone, of any age or gender, undertaking any activity. In this first chapter, I'll share with you what the Performance Equation reveals about how the deployment of our focus of attention directly influences our ability to perform. It will explain why the *target* of our focus has such a powerful influence on our performance and shed light on the most common error that we all make virtually every day.

By understanding how these pieces fit together, you'll become more effective in controlling your thoughts so that they can be directed to the right thing at the right time. You'll also be in a better position to teach your child how to control their thinking in the most challenging situations, and by doing so, you'll arm them with one of the most important life skills they could ever possess.

In Part One, I'll discuss the seven key Rules of the Mental Road. Using this simple framework of basic rules, we'll examine how our mind works in straightforward, practical terms and consider how this way of thinking affects our personal performance.

In Part Two, I'll address the question: "So now that I understand how I mentally sabotage my own performance, how do I change and how, ultimately, can I help my child to change?" The A.C.T. Model process will answer these specific questions. It's a proven process that I've successfully delivered with world champions, high-performance athletes, and numerous other top-level professionals over many years. In fact, top performers in many areas *rely* on their personal A.C.T. Model to guide their thinking when they need to generate their best performances. This process blends the best elements from a number of recognized psychological- and mental-training techniques and offers a practical yet simple methodology to help you deliberately shape and control your dominant thought. With improved control, your mindset will consistently be more positive and task-focused, whether things are going well or not. Furthermore, once you understand how to establish and implement this process for yourself, you'll be in a better position to teach its basic tenets to your child.

The A.C.T. Model process is simply a tool, but I believe this is the most important contribution this book might possibly make. I can't overstate this enough. If you incorporate the A.C.T. Model process into your life and teach its basic principles to your child, you'll be well on your way to gaining that elusive yet critical mental skill that all high-performance people constantly seek—that of *mental toughness.* If you model the process consistently and attempt to integrate it into your own life on a day-to-day basis, not only will you develop a set of mental skills that will serve you well both in the competitive world and in life in general, but by your example, you'll also teach your child to do the same. As most of us probably realize, in many situations *we* are our own worst enemy and what we really need to do is learn how to get out of our own way. Children are really no different from us in this regard. If you can teach them how to direct and control their thoughts, they can learn how to more effectively perform "in the moment." In so doing, they'll be better able to express the full extent of their talents, unencumbered by the destructive mindset that so often grips us all as we face our most significant and challenging obstacles.

As we prepare to take this journey together, consider what it would mean to you if you were able to consistently control your thoughts in such a way that you *allow yourself* to deliver your very best performance in the face of every major challenge that you undertake in life (e.g., the "big" meeting, the "big" event, the "big" game, etc.). Consider the lifelong effect on your child that would accrue if you teach them to understand these principles in their early years. What a gift you would be offering them for their lifetime! Just imagine the possibilities. . . .

CHAPTER 1

The Performance Equation: A Simple Framework for Performance Thinking

"A" × "B" = RESULTS

THE ROOT OF THE PROBLEM

Sometimes our performance can only be described as spectacular—moments of brilliance where everything just goes right! Our focus is on target and our mind is sharp, easily processing the information that allows us to bring our "A" Game to whatever it is that we're doing. We possess a relaxed confidence, and this powerful mindset facilitates our ability to effectively deal with any challenge or problem that arises. We can almost tell what's going to happen before it does. It's almost like being clairvoyant. Our performance feels effortless even though our energy level and effort are indeed high. It's one of those all-too-rare "YES!" moments. We're in our mental "Zone" of best performance.

But then again, sometimes we're not. . . .

Why is it that, in some situations, our performance truly is the best that we're capable of delivering, while in others, we struggle and just can't seem to get into the mental groove where we do our best work? We've all experienced situations when our ability to perform a task that we may even know well varies, sometimes even dramatically. We can't always put our finger on why it happens, but we do understand that it's *not* because we forget from one time to the next what it takes to execute perfectly. There's something else going on here.

In this chapter, I'm going to share information with you that I believe will reveal at least part of the answer to this conundrum. In so doing, I'm confident you'll come to recognize that the fundamental and somewhat universal reason we experience these major swings in personal performance lies in our inconsistent application of *the one key basic mental skill* that truly underlies our ability to perform. This occurs whether the performance is in the office, on the playing field, in the classroom, on stage, or wherever.

When my clients participate in my comprehensive individual performance program, I ask every one of these high performers what they hope to gain from the experience. Stated another way, I'm interested to know what they feel most often holds them back when it comes time for them to "deliver" in their moment of performance. Stop and take a few moments before you read on to reflect on the following two questions with respect to yourself:

What sometimes stops me from delivering my best performance when it's "go" time?

In the final moment, what gets in my way and damages the mindset that leads me to deliver my best performance?

Would it surprise you to find out that more than 90% of my high-performance clients reply to these questions with at least one of the same two answers, and often with both? It doesn't matter what profession or sport they're involved in, what culture they're from, what language they speak, whether they're male or female, or how old they are; virtually every one of these high performers are looking for the same key things. You might also find it revealing that in every group seminar I've ever conducted (in the world of sport and beyond), these same two issues are consistently identified as key elements within the first minute of being asked the question. The two main requests that I've consistently heard from these highly successful performers over the years have been:

1. "Show me how to maintain my *confidence* when things aren't going well, because when my confidence slips and I start to doubt myself or feel as though I might fail, my performance goes down."
2. "Show me how to *focus* more effectively and when I lose my focus, how to get it back quickly, because when I'm distracted by something and am not task-focused, I don't do my best work."

Isn't it interesting? It doesn't matter what "business" they're in; the same two issues appear to be centrally important to their ability to deliver their best performance. In fact, these two requests provide us with a powerful clue to one of the fundamental secrets behind both why high-performance people become successful and also how each one of us ultimately sabotages our own performance. Let's examine these two issues more deeply to see if we can understand the root of the problem.

"Show me how to maintain my confidence when things aren't going well."

How is it that many of the most successful athletes, performers, and business professionals out there today sometimes wrestle with this issue of self-confidence? Are these not some of the most confident individuals you can think of? And yet, when we drill down to the core of it, my forty years of experience in the high-performance world affirms that this remains an issue that they still don't always have a good handle on. While it isn't always the case, at some points in their lives and in some challenging situations, the problem of self-doubt corrupts their ability to deliver their best performance. Should it really surprise the rest of us then that we too sometimes find ourselves wrestling with this very same issue?

It would be interesting to know how many of you responded to the questions I posed earlier with answers that sound something like this: fear of failure, self-doubt, lack of confidence, worry over not being good enough, etc. My guess is that if you're being honest, a significant number of you probably did, because confidence appears to be a basic issue that almost everybody wrestles with, at least at some times and in some situations.

Do you think that children are any different from us adults in this regard? Have you observed any evidence that might suggest that they too wrestle with this problem of lack of confidence? My observations over the years suggest that the answer is a resounding YES. But when we examine the issue more deeply, we come to realize that it wasn't always this way.

Anyone who has cared for an infant will recognize the absolutely fearless nature of that child as they first begin to crawl, stand, and then later take their first steps. They're not wasting time or energy doubting themselves or worrying about failure; they simply engage each new task and give it their best shot. If they slip and fall, as long as they don't physically hurt themselves, their natural instinct is to just get back up and try again. This fearless, task-focused mindset supports their ability to forge ahead and acquire new, important skills. There comes a time, however—not too far along in their young life, in fact—when their focus fundamentally changes, and they begin to fret more over difficulties and worry that they might not be up to the task. That's when the self-confidence they showed as infants begins to slip through their fingers and this self-doubt corrupts their ability to perform at their best, or even sometimes to perform at all:

- The child who's afraid to even try riding a two-wheeled bicycle (even though it may have training wheels) due to a fear of falling, hurting themselves, and not being able to master the skill.

- The young gymnast who's afraid to try a new move due to a fear of not succeeding, with all of the attendant consequences they perceive that failure might bring—getting hurt, looking like an uncoordinated boob, being laughed at by their peers, etc.
- The child who's terrified to speak in front of the class because they fear they might make a fool of themselves if they make a mistake or "freeze up."
- The student who's afraid to sign up for the spelling bee or a math competition because they're afraid they aren't good enough to win, even though they may be a top student.
- The adult who's afraid to take on a project around the house because they fear they won't be successful in executing it properly, even though it's fully within their skill set to accomplish.
- And so on.

What's changed? Is this *fear of failure* a learned behavior or is it simply a natural progression of thought that's hardwired into our brain, following a master plan set out in our DNA? I believe that this response is more of a learned behavior.

I'd like you to take a few moments to think about and answer the following questions as they pertain to you:

- What are the circumstances around which you generally begin to doubt yourself?
- What is it that damages your confidence in the moment when you're called upon to perform?
- When you engage a challenging task, what is your greatest fear?

Of course, I can't know how you will respond to these three simple questions, but I'm willing to bet that my guess isn't far off. When I've asked these questions of my clients and the many people I've encountered over the years in my work, they invariably respond with something that sounds like this: "I start to doubt myself and become tentative when I fear that I won't be up to the challenge and that I might fail . . . and my confidence then seems to go out the window."

The simple truth is that the vast majority of people allow their confidence to be defined by the results they achieve (or fail to achieve). When results are good, it's relatively easy for them to maintain a high level of self-confidence. When results are poor, however, their confidence often takes a beating and their personal performance usually suffers. When my clients ask, "Show me how to maintain my confidence when things aren't going well," their question actually gives us insight into the underlying problem that they're wrestling with. They too often allow their confidence to be defined by the outcome of their actions: where a good outcome leads to good confidence and a poor outcome leads to poor confidence. They recognize that this tight connection between confidence and results puts them on a roller coaster of emotion because they know that they won't always get the results that they're hoping for. They're trying to find a way to disconnect these two variables (results and confidence) from each other so that the one (results) doesn't have so much of a powerful influence on the other (confidence).

The basic problem with this logic is that as long as we insist on defining our confidence around results, we'll never be able to get a solid handle on this issue of self-confidence. That's because the truth of the matter is that we can't actually control results. ***No matter how much we wish we could, we ultimately can't control the outcome.*** The extension of this argument is that, since we can't control the outcome, we'll never be able to control our level of confidence if we allow these two elements to remain intrinsically connected to one another.

Now, if results didn't matter, we wouldn't have much of a problem, but of course they do. For some of my clients, results matter so much that, for them, results represent the difference between living and dying. For the rest of us, the consequences of our actions aren't as final perhaps, but they can nonetheless be significant. We're compensated on the basis of the results we generate, we're promoted at work or school on the basis of our success, and we may even lose our job or fail to graduate if results (or acceptable test scores) aren't forthcoming. Even our self-esteem—the reputation that we develop with ourselves over our lifetime—is affected by the results we achieve. We think more highly of ourselves when we're successful and think less of ourselves when we're not.

For children, results are just as important to them as they are to us adults. Their goals aren't really that different from our own, since the things that are uppermost in their minds are similar to those that we consider important: to be liked, to be accepted by our peers, not to disappoint the important people in our lives, to be successful in the meaningful things we undertake, to be seen as "cool," etc. We all want good results, and we all want to avoid bad ones. I've never had a single person in my work life over the years come to me and say, "I want to be a loser," or "I really hope that I fail." I doubt that you have either.

While everyone wants to be successful, I've certainly met people from three distinct groups who aren't there yet. The first group is comprised of people who simply don't know how to be successful. They haven't been taught the process that can lead them to success, but once they know how to go about it, they're willing and able to engage that process diligently and with tenacity and, more often than not, they do become successful.

The second group is comprised of people who don't truly believe they *can* be successful. These people don't have faith in themselves, in their ability to forge ahead and overcome the obstacles they perceive will likely block their path. Perhaps their family culture of constant criticism leads them to believe that success for them is unlikely because they don't have the "stuff" that champions need to be successful. These people face a greater challenge since they first must come to believe that they can be successful before they firmly engage the process that's likely to take them there.

Then there's the third group. These are the people who simply aren't willing to put in the effort necessary to become successful. For whatever reason, the reward for these individuals just isn't worth the effort they perceive is needed, and they prefer to aim low and coast through life at a modest level. For some, they may even be happy at times going through life this way, although they still sure wish they could be more successful, with everything that success brings.

Over the years, I've used a simple equation (I call it the **Performance Equation**) to help explain to my clients how what we focus on factors into the generation of results. The equation is useful because it directly addresses both of these central issues of confidence and focus.

"A" × "B" = Results

In this equation, the **"Results"** that each of us accomplishes are the product of two variables: **"A"** and **"B."** Let's decompose this equation by substituting the phrase "My Performance" for the "A" variable in the equation and the phrase "All the Factors Outside of My Control" for the "B" variable. Keep in mind that this equation isn't intended to be taken literally as a mathematical expression—it's a conceptual one. It now reads:

"My Performance" × "All the Factors Outside of My Control" = Results

My Performance—which is defined by the skill, the experience, the talent, and the knowledge that I possess at the moment of that performance, together with the commitment and effort I invest to deliver it in that moment—is only *one* of the variables that influences the results I'm capable of achieving as I tackle the many challenges of my life. Other "B" factors that are truly outside of my control (such as what my competitors or other people might do, what others might choose to think, marketplace forces over which I have no control, equipment failure, legislative regulations, luck, etc.) can and often do have a direct influence on the results that I'm able to achieve in a given situation. If you think about the world of competition, for example, as soon as we introduce a single other competitor into the mix, we've introduced an automatic "B" factor into our results' equation. The reason is quite simply that we can't control what that opponent might choose to do. It's part of life—sometimes we're the windshield and sometimes we're the bug, and in some instances, things that are outside of our control (both fortunate and unfortunate) simply happen.

If we carry this argument further, this means that in some situations, even though our performance is truly the best that we're capable of in that moment, we may still not be successful in achieving the results we hoped for. A full-on "A" Game performance doesn't always yield the outcome we're shooting for. If it did, the Performance Equation would read "A" = Results. But it doesn't. And yet, we're taught (and, in turn, we teach our children) that hard work and perseverance will always lead to success. The harsh reality, however, is that this isn't always the case, and to some degree, we sell this false notion of "hard work = success" in order to motivate our children to work hard. We tell them "If you work hard, you will be successful" because we know that hard work is almost always needed to create success.

We tend to gloss over the fact that sometimes, even though they might work very hard indeed, they won't always be successful in achieving what they'd hoped to achieve because they won't be able to overcome the "B" factors in that situation, or their knowledge or skill level at that time may simply not be up to the challenge. These are the facts. Just because we work hard and give our all to the challenge, it doesn't mean that we necessarily will always be successful. Sometimes we work hard and with diligence, but we still fail to generate the results we're striving for. I'm confident that based on your own experience, as well as looking at the experiences of others around you, you know this to be true.

This doesn't mean, however, that we shouldn't draw the connection between hard work and success with our children, but rather, that we shouldn't draw it too directly in any kind of a cause-and-effect relationship. Otherwise, we have a difficult time explaining to them why, in many instances where they've given their all and worked hard, they may not have achieved the results they'd hoped to achieve . . . and our argument loses some persuasiveness and credibility. We should most definitely teach them that there is a solid link between hard work, perseverance, and success, but also help them to understand that these do not guarantee the outcome that we want.

Believing that you *can* be successful as you undertake a challenge is of critical importance, because if you don't believe that you can be successful, it's unlikely that you will be. If you don't believe that you can be successful, it's much easier to give up at the first significant roadblock you encounter. If, on the other hand, you believe that success is possible, you're more likely to persevere and push through the obstacles that might temporarily impede progress toward your goal. This is the relationship that you want your children to understand more clearly. Working hard and persevering in the face of adversity *increases the likelihood* of their being successful in achieving their goals, even though it's not a guarantee. If we teach them that they can often push through adversity and, by being correctly focused and working hard, they can create new opportunities for success, we'll arm our children with a strong set of life skills that are based on an accurate understanding of the relationship between their individual performance (the "A" in our equation) and the success (Results) that they can achieve.

We need to be careful, however, to teach our children to avoid creating the *expectation* that a certain outcome will be realized in advance of their performance because this can actually get in the way of their delivering that performance. Sometimes, the expectation forms because input by others leads us to believe that a positive outcome is a "sure thing." In other instances, it can arise as a natural follow-on to good prior results. When you've done really well in practice and have been at the top of the results table in the preliminary rounds, how common do you think it is to expect things to continue to go well in the next session or game? It's very common, based on my experience, and this poses no immediate problem if things go our way and we end up being successful. In fact, these "I knew I would win!" situations tend to reinforce our belief that an expectation of success is a good thing, because if we go into the challenge with an expectation of success, success will necessarily find its way to our door. We tend to think of this as the power of positive thought.

But what happens to our thinking with this mindset of expectation if things don't go our way (and how often does that happen, right?). While we're engaged in the task, what happens if we begin to perceive or observe that things aren't going according to our set of prior outcome expectations? It doesn't matter that the reason behind the lack of a good result may be because of problems on our part (perhaps we're delivering an "A minus" performance today because we're fatigued, distracted, worried, etc.) or due to something that's completely outside of our control (a true "B minus" factor). In these situations where things start to go wrong, we tend to mentally disconnect from the process of what we're doing. Our focus of attention typically shifts away from execution related to the task in which we're engaged and is redirected to the growing gap between where we perceive we are relative to where we expected (or hoped) to be.

We begin to worry about the fact that the results that we're hoping for—or were expecting—seem to be slipping through our fingers and our anxiety increases as we begin to fear that we might actually fail. All the while, our focus tends to remain firmly affixed, at least in part, on the gap between where we are versus where we want to be in order to monitor whether things are getting better or worse. Of course the problem becomes greater as the gap gets larger, because instead of focusing fully on the process of what we're doing, we end up focusing more and more on the result of our actions (or in this case, the lack of results we perceive are unfolding in front of our very eyes). A poor performance then often becomes a self-fulfilling prophecy. I refer to this problem with my clients as the Demon of Expectations! Quite simply put, when the Demon of Expectations rears its ugly head, we tend to focus more on *how* we're doing rather than on *what* we're doing and this always ends up hurting our performance, because we're simply focused on the wrong thing.

The natural response in situations where things aren't going our way is either to give up or to try to close the gap to make up the ground we've lost, because the expectation of success we created in our mind before the event is still hanging out there. In the performance world, this mindset often leads to catastrophic results because the individual often responds by "overdriving" the situation. They try too hard and push to force something to happen. Patience goes out the window, and errors in execution are more likely to occur because they're focused on the wrong thing . . . the Result. This will become even clearer to you when we address Rule #2 in the Rules of the Mental Road later in the book.

Let me share with you a real-world example to illustrate how the Demon of Expectations can take hold of not only the performance of an individual but also that of an entire team. Many years ago, I attended an elite-level soccer tournament of high-school-aged boys. Based on prior season performance, there was a team in the tournament that was touted as being a shoo-in for the overall win since they'd been undefeated all season long in their division. It was a generally accepted expectation.

In the early games, they demonstrated why some people might have thought this way—they played a disciplined game and their players showed excellent fitness and technical skills. In the quarter-finals, however, I observed a growing cockiness (some might even call it arrogance) that was shared not only among the players but within the coaching staff as well. Their play shifted to a more risk-oriented one because they seemed to think they could do no wrong. They went on to win the game . . . as they had expected. I found this quite interesting but developed an uneasy feeling that it might lead to trouble later on.

As they rolled into their semifinal game, that cockiness seemed to manifest itself even before they took to the field. It didn't look like they were taking the game very seriously even though the opposing team had a strong record as well. In the early part of the game, the play was somewhat even and solid attempts on goal were made by both sides. At one point, however, the opposing team made an excellent series of plays and took the lead by a goal after having elegantly outplayed the backfield players. Nothing seemed to be too out of place as the game forged ahead. However, only a few minutes later, the opposing team scored another quick goal—due in part to a lucky break on their behalf—to take a 2–0 lead in the game.

The wheels began to fall off the wagon, and the tone on the field changed instantly. It was evident from the way the top-seeded team's players communicated with each other (as well as how the coaches communicated with the players) that their collective anxiety spiked. The communication became more aggressive and intolerant of perceived errors as players criticized each other, and what was a previously disciplined team suddenly became a group of frantic players who seemed to forget where they were supposed to be on the field. They also got caught out making more and more mistakes. At one point, I heard a player yell out, "Come on, you guys! We're supposed to win this thing!" The team ultimately lost 4–1 in what was considered a major upset in that the number-one-seeded team never even made it to the finals of the tournament. Their expectation of success was derailed by circumstances, and the more in trouble they found themselves, the more they focused on the trouble they were in, and the majority of players on that team mentally sabotaged themselves in that semifinal game.

It's a simple but sometimes hard to accept fact that we can't control results because we can't control the "B" factors in the Performance Equation. By definition, these are the factors that exist outside of our direct control. And yet, the vast majority of people (of all ages, genders, and cultures) insist on defining their confidence around the results they achieve. This is why we tend to have high levels of confidence when results are good and also why we tend to lose confidence and worry about failing when results are poor, or when we perceive that the challenge is beyond our capacity to meet it. When our confidence is eroded, our focus of attention shifts away from the task we're engaged in to be redirected to the source of our worry or fear. Our anxiety then increases because of this worry and uncertainty, and our thoughts lock onto the perceived negative consequences of our impending failure. Does this sound like something you may have experienced yourself in the past? I know I have.

The sad irony implicit in this argument is that the more we focus on the outcome of what we're doing while we're engaged in the action of doing it, the less likely we are to do it well. The reason for this is that we're fundamentally focusing on the wrong thing, and Rule #2 of the Mental Road explains exactly why this is true. *The mind can only actively process one thought at a time.* Alternatively, the more we focus our attention on the task in which we're engaged, fully connected to what we're doing in the moment that we're doing it, the better our performance tends to be . . . and the results that come from that performance generally look after themselves. But often, because results are so darned important, we tend to fixate on and worry about the results of our actions rather than focus effectively on the process that will take us there. We know this to be true from experience, and this is the basis of the modern philosophy of thought revolving around the importance of being mentally "present."

To reframe this issue another way, consider the following scenario. Let's assume that you are tasked with taking on an important challenge. It could be a major work presentation to your colleagues or clients, a performance on stage that you've been rehearsing for weeks, a difficult surgery you must perform on a severely injured patient who ends up in your emergency room, or a penalty kick for your team that will determine whether you win or lose the game and go on to the finals, etc. It doesn't really matter what the task might be; suffice it to say that it's something that's really important to you. Allow me to propose a sequence of thoughts that wouldn't be unreasonable for most people to go through in such a situation.

In the lead up to this big event, your mind is occupied with thinking about what you have to do and all of the work (training, research, prepping materials, etc.) that must be completed in order to be ready to bring your best performance to the task. It might even feel somewhat overwhelming to you as all of the things you must do swirl around wildly in your mind. You become a little like the squirrel in the road, not knowing where to focus because you're trying to focus everywhere at the same time and you simply can't.

But how many of us would also get caught up worrying about the outcome of our actions? Results are important, right? People are counting on us to get the job done and to get it done correctly. We don't want to let important people down after all. If we're not successful (if we fail), what are the consequences of this failure? Preparation time for most people is usually occupied by a mix of focusing on the task at hand and worrying, to some greater or lesser degree, about the consequences of not getting it done to the level that we hope. Then we go about engaging the task.

Once engaged, we manage to direct our focus of attention to the task in front of us and work the "process" that we established as we were preparing for this moment. While we're actually engaged in the doing, however, our focus occasionally shifts to think about how we think we're doing. We check in on the results as they appear to be unfolding before us by watching our audience for signs or clues about how things are going. If we perceive that things are going according to plan and we believe that a good outcome is likely, we tend to relax more and just work our process because the results seem to be looking after themselves.

However, if our ongoing "checkup" suggests that things are not going according to plan (e.g., the bosses don't seem happy with what we've presented thus far; we've made a couple of mistakes in the musical piece we're playing and we perceive a level of dissatisfaction from the audience; the damage is more extensive than we had anticipated and the patient's vital signs are becoming dangerously unstable; etc.), our mind can become overridden by negative thoughts that are associated with failure. When this happens, our anxiety spikes and we tend to become fixated on the difficulties and the problems we're having rather than being focused on our actions in the moment that will yield the best result possible under the circumstances.

I realize I'm speaking in generalities here because no single example can drive the point home for everyone, but I hope this discussion can help you to connect the dots on how the nature of *what we focus on* has a significant effect on our ability to perform. The mindset I've described above is just as prevalent in children who undertake important challenges in their life—at school, on the playground, at home, and in personal relationships they have with important people in their life.

I'd like to take a few moments now to address the issue of *adversity* and perhaps put a different spin on it for you to consider.

Adversity is one of the greatest constants in life, and it ultimately affects everyone at some point. Quite often, adversity simply exists as a "B minus" factor—something over which we have no direct control. It's probably accurate to say that most things that are important and meaningful to the human species require dedication, commitment, and hard work to achieve. But our children have become accustomed to instant gratification—text messaging, smart phones, online shopping, the microwave oven, any information they might want at their fingertips via the Internet—and anything less than immediate is unacceptable. But life is not paved with moments of instant gratification the way that kids often see it, because anything of real substance takes time and effort to acquire. Otherwise, real success would be easy and everyone would be successful, wouldn't they? Often, we encounter adversity as we work toward our goals, and life throws what seems to be an unending array of challenges and roadblocks in our path.

It's not just us though. Our children also face adversity virtually every day as they strive to accomplish the things that are important to them. Recognizing this, our natural tendency as parents is to protect our children from adversity, to prevent them from struggling and getting hurt, both physically and emotionally. We want to spare them the difficult mental and emotional turmoil that's an inherent part of struggle and failure. It's probably one of the strongest natural instincts we possess as a species—the desire to protect our young. We work hard to give them more than we had when we were growing up and to pave the way for them to enjoy a positive and secure future. But if we're not careful, there can be potential unintended consequences on their growth and development of this natural drive we have to protect them. Here's what I've observed over the years working with younger athletes.

You may have heard the term "helicopter parents" used to describe parents who "hover" over their children, who watch them like a hawk so that the child won't stumble and fall or hurt themselves in any way. They try to protect the child from any kind of failure or emotional distress. They fill their child's spare time with organized activities and allow very few opportunities for free play. They step in to resolve their child's conflicts at school and on the playground and make excuses for them when they do fail (and they all do fail, at times). They insist on showering them with praise, even if they didn't do a very good job at what they were doing and the praise wasn't warranted. At the extreme, these are the parents who believe that performance shouldn't be scored, that everyone should get a ribbon or trophy, that a pass/fail grade is the only thing that we should provide in order to allow these kids to continue to feel good about themselves in this difficult and challenging world that is fraught with setbacks. They step in at the first sign of struggle to "fix" the problem and negotiate a result for their child.

What do you think the children of these parents learn from this behavior? What are their parents teaching them by their day-to-day example?

In my experience, these children generally don't develop strong coping skills and their mental skills overall are weak. Their attention span is usually not very good because they respond like the squirrel in the road—with their focus of attention constantly scattered by the sensory-information overload that they've become accustomed to. They don't manage challenges particularly well, and they get stressed out more easily in moments of adversity. They don't *trust* in themselves to be able to move past the challenge and come out the other side. Their self-esteem can sometimes be low because someone has always been there to clean up their mess or fix their boo-boos and they've never developed a sense of confidence in themselves because they haven't been given the chance to face and learn to overcome significant difficulties. As a result, they're fearful of any new endeavor that they must face as they get older.

If children are always praised, even when they deliver a mediocre performance, they tend to overestimate their abilities in a nonrealistic way and never have the desire to learn what they can do better. They come to believe that they can do no wrong and that they are always "on their game" even when they're not, and they can't handle critique. Because they've been told they're "special" their whole life, they insist on being treated as special even if they're not. Some of them don't even know how to go about picking themselves up after a major failure and refocusing on the task at hand because they've never had to do it before. They adopt a "woe is me" attitude and need to be led by the hand. They haven't developed their "tenacity" muscle because they've never had to persevere through temporary failures and setbacks.

When they get beyond the reach of their parents (as they grow older and move out on their own), they become easily distressed by failure or setbacks. They need to be emotionally "propped up" by their friends, teachers, coaches, and bosses with a regular diet of "at-a-boy" praise to keep them working on task and to help them avoid becoming depressed and feeling unfulfilled because they haven't made their first million by age thirty-five or found their perfect mate by their early twenties. They require ongoing praise from the people around them because this is what gives them validation, not the internal knowledge that they delivered their best effort and their best work. Obviously, this isn't true of every young person, but if you ask older workers from a previous generation about their view of the younger generation of employees they encounter, this picture is unfortunately not uncommon.

This isn't the real world though. It certainly isn't the world that I work in. In the high-performance world, these individuals are quickly left by the wayside since overcoming adversity is the order of the day. You're defined by your actions and the things you achieve, and how you bounce back from the difficulties and successes you experience in life define who you are. If you don't have the spine to take a beating (in some cases, literally) and get back up and dive into the challenge again, you'll never likely be successful because success lies at the end of a road that is almost always paved with adversity and hard work.

In my opinion, while we certainly don't want to allow children to get hurt in any kind of meaningful or permanent way, allowing them to face adversity and, yes, even to fail as young children is a *good* and *desirable* thing. With the right kind of coaching, these experiences can become great teaching moments for us and learning moments for them. But this, of course, requires us to be fully engaged as parents—taking the time out of our busy day to really communicate with our kids to help them put their successes and failures into context within their lives. If we do so in a meaningful way, we can use these moments to underscore that the practice of pushing through adversity and overcoming the challenge through determination and hard work is what will arm them with the most important life skills they'll ever need. This is what creates mental and emotional resilience, and this is one of the key characteristics exhibited by successful people.

So how can we go about transferring this understanding to our children? I offer these following suggestions as food for thought:

- Help your child to understand that, in the moment, *they can't do better than the best they can do.* Nobody can. From the time that they're toddlers and beyond, reinforce this message with age-appropriate language.
- As they grow, remind them they can't control results. Help them to understand that because they can't, there's no benefit to them in worrying over results (the basic premise of the "A" × "B" = Results equation).
- Draw the important connections between effort, commitment, and perseverance and celebrate *these behaviors* when your child demonstrates them because these are the precursors of success.
- Help your child to understand that happiness isn't created in a vacuum. It's the by-product of living a meaningful life, where they are fully engaged in fulfilling activities and relationships.
- Help your child to clarify their goals and define an action plan to move them in that direction, and then guide them to execute their plan in a focused, reasonable way.
- If they didn't exhibit "A" Game behaviors because they were lazy, distracted, etc., let them know that this is something they can change to be better the next time and help them to understand that this will increase the likelihood of their achieving their goals.

- If the results happen to be good, celebrate those too (because that's the goal, after all), but even within these moments of success, remind them in a positive way that the results they achieve in the different things they undertake are a product of their actions, influenced by the things they can't control.

- If a "B" factor temporarily derails the achievement of their goal, ensure that they keep a healthy *perspective* on that failure to understand that it may only be temporary and that it may have had *nothing* to do with them but, rather, with something that was outside of their control. Just because they failed to achieve their goal now doesn't mean that it should terminate the pursuit of their goal in the future.

- If the failure was partly related to the fact that they didn't do a good job, offer specific suggestions in a nonconfrontational way for how they could make it better next time, as opposed to criticism for not having achieved some expected result. Critique their performance but avoid criticizing them as individuals. If all you offer is criticism (which attaches a value judgment)—even though you intend it to help—you're helping them to crush their own self-esteem.

- Motivate them to dive back into the challenge again and work hard to deliver the best performance they can the next time. Help them to redirect their focus on the process of what they're trying to do and let the results look after themselves.

- Encourage them to understand that just because they may have failed at something doesn't mean that *they* are a failure. In fact, they may have done a great job and that's worth celebrating, regardless of the outcome (as long as they *did* indeed do a good job). This will help them over time to break the link between confidence and results that grips most people and will allow them to develop a sense of confidence in their own ability to fully engage the challenges in life—win, lose, or draw. They'll surely be disappointed about lousy results when they do occur, but the reality of poor results won't corrupt their self-confidence or the mindset that they adopt in challenging situations since they'll clearly come to understand how these pieces fit together. They need to realize that the notion that "you can do anything that you put your mind to" isn't necessarily true if your immediate goals are actually unrealistic.

I believe that the most important piece in the performance puzzle lies in their gaining a clear understanding of how the way they direct their focus of attention has a significant influence on their performance as well as, ultimately, on results. The key is correct focus. It's important that their goals be clear in their mind but also that they understand (and emotionally accept) that the best results come from simply focusing on the process involved in the execution of whatever they're doing in the moment when they're doing it.

A side benefit of instilling this way of thinking in your child's mind is that this philosophy will make it much easier for them to learn how to remain calm in the face of adversity and it will effectively neutralize anxiety, because they'll learn to stop focusing on (and worrying about) results and their consequences. Instead, they'll come to focus deliberately on what they can control, and as long as they're fully focused on the task in front of them, there will be no mental-processing capacity assigned to worry. That's because worry only surfaces when we disconnect from what we're actually doing (the action) and instead shift our thoughts to the *consequences* of our actions. This is why correct focus on the task, together with a strong sense of confidence in our own ability to engage it while delivering the best that we're capable of, is so fundamentally critical to the mindset that allows us to create and deliver our highest-quality performances. I'm confident that your children will come to understand this if you make the case over time in a consistent manner—it all depends on the way you frame the relationship between their performance and the results they achieve.

If you're looking for a simple script to guide your thoughts as well as the input you offer your children, consider this short recipe:

1. Remain calm, because when your mind is calm and clear, it's easier to make good decisions.
2. Adopt a singular focus on the task in front of you.
3. Commit to a full-on effort because success most often requires effort and commitment.
4. Be prepared to struggle and persevere in the face of adversity, because there is bound to be some. "B" factors simply happen as a normal part of life.
5. Again, *control* your focus so that it's directed fully to the task in front of you—to the right thing at the right time.
6. *Trust* in the fundamental truth of the "A" × "B" = Results equation, and let the results look after themselves. Focus on what you can control.

While this recipe doesn't guarantee that your children will be successful, it does increase the likelihood that they'll develop and sustain a mindset that supports their ability to deliver their best performance. This, in turn, will optimize their success in any task in which they're engaged. The key is to help them to understand that the likelihood of achieving their goals is greatest when they focus effectively on what they're doing in the moment they're doing it. It's about process, and it's a little like driving in fog. When it's foggy, you can only see a short way but as long as you know in what direction you're headed and focus on the road immediately in front of you, you can drive a long way and get to your destination using this approach.

In the following section, I provide an overview of the simple framework I refer to as the Rules of the Mental Road. In subsequent chapters, we'll turn our attention to understanding the meaning of each rule and how they're interrelated.

AN OVERVIEW

The Seven Key Rules of the Mental Road

Rule #1 If you want to climb out of a hole, the very first thing you must do is *stop digging!*

Sometimes we dig ourselves into a mental hole by thinking negative thoughts. These negative thoughts gain strength and power the more we mentally process them, and before we know it, we're staring at the bottom of a hole and "digging" furiously. We end up so far down that hole of negative thinking that we can't seem to find our way out. If you want to shift your mindset to positive and task-focused thinking, you first must *choose* to process only positive and task-focused thoughts. If you don't consciously, actively, and deliberately take control of your thought process and stop the mental digging, you won't be able to shift your dominant thought to the kind of positive and task-focused thinking you need to turn yourself around and climb out of the hole.

Rule #2 The mind can only actively process ONE thought *at a time.*

No matter how hard you try to think about two thoughts *at the same time,* you can't do it. No one can actively process two thoughts at the same time even though we are able to shift back and forth from one thought to another in a multitasking mode. What's the implication of this rule from a performance point of view? It's simple but powerful: If you're focused on this (whatever "this" is), you can't be focused on that (whatever "that" is) *at the same moment in time.* Herein lies the secret to generating your best performance!

Rule #3 You can't *NOT* think about whatever is on your mind.

What generally happens when you tell yourself not to get nervous, not to get angry, or not to mess up? Quite often, exactly what you wanted *not* to do is exactly what you do, exactly the way you pictured it in your mind's eye! That's because your mind *can't act positively* in response to a negative thought. Think about this carefully: What's the consequence of flooding your mind with negative thoughts? The answer: You become negative, and this impacts your performance in a negative way. Since you can't *not* think about whatever's on your mind, it's essential that you learn to effectively control your dominant thought to direct it to what's immediately relevant at that moment.

Rule #4 Your *dominant thought* determines your emotions, the behaviors that flow from those emotions, and ultimately, your ability to perform.

Your dominant thought is translated into action through the work of your unconscious mind. This is why imagery is such a powerful tool in shaping our emotions, our behaviors, and ultimately, our ability to perform. Often, however, we implant dominant thoughts in our mind that are negative and counterproductive to our performance. Rule #3 reminds us that we *can't not think* about whatever thought is dominant within our mind. You must ensure that the *dominant thought* you choose to focus on is one that will contribute to your ability to perform, rather than take away from it.

Rule #5 You *ARE in control* of your dominant thought.

We can't often control the events that occur around us (like winning or what others might think or do), but we're always 100% in control of *how we choose to see and respond to* the situation in front of us. We can choose to spin out of control and focus on the negatives, or we can "reframe" the event and look for the opportunity in it. As we get older, we come to know that, in many instances, there is opportunity in those situations if we look for it. Even in the most difficult circumstances, the situation always presents itself as an opportunity to measure ourselves against difficult challenges, to rise to the occasion, to exhibit a champion's mindset, and to learn from the experience.

Rule #6 Your *perception* or *perspective* regarding the challenges that you face will determine your dominant thought.

It's not the challenging events in our life that cause us stress, it's our interpretation (our perception or perspective) regarding those events that leads to a stress response that can be negative and counterproductive to our performance or positive, to energize and motivate us to put in the focus and effort needed to bring about our best performance. Perception ultimately takes place in the brain, not in the eyes. Therefore, what we see is our mind's interpretation of what's actually there. If we help our children to change their perspective regarding the challenges that they face on a daily basis, they'll change their dominant thought. Their stress response will be reduced and their performance will be optimized . . . just like for us.

The glass of water that one person sees as being half-empty is the same glass that another person sees as being half-full. It's a matter of perspective. An active and purposeful *shift in your thinking* can have a positive effect on your performance and your health. It is important that you choose your perspective carefully!

Rule #7 If you do what you've always done,
you'll get what you've always gotten . . .
If you want something different,
you must approach the challenges you face
with a different mindset!

This one doesn't need any explanation, does it?

PART ONE

The Seven Key Rules of the Mental Road

Even though my vocation provides me with the opportunity to work one on one with high performers in the "real world," I view my role simply as that of an educator. Ultimately, I believe that if I can teach my clients how to bait their hook and cast their line with precision, they'll learn how to fish successfully on their own. While I try to play a supporting role as they work to implement this way of thinking into their lives and their work—especially in the early stages of the skill-acquisition process—once they understand the basic principles regarding how we mentally process information and how this processing either supports our ability to perform or sabotages it, they're well on their way to understanding how to optimize their own performance. Then, with a simple but powerful tool like the A.C.T. Model process, they can begin to systematically take control of and reprogram their way of thinking to realize all the benefits that this Performance Thinking approach brings about.

Many years ago, I created the Rules of the Mental Road as a basic framework to serve as the backbone upon which to build this educational process. While the rules are simple—and I suspect that some people might even consider them to be "simplistic"—they have proven to be powerful because they speak to how the way we mentally process information directly influences the quality of our personal performance. I formulated these rules based upon my personal observations over the years and on background information from the scientific literature. Over the decades, these rules have proven to be:

- *Fundamental,* in that they're simple and underlie the thought process that either allows us to perform to the best of our ability or sabotages us as we engage in the performance itself.
- *Universal,* because they apply to everyone. It doesn't matter what culture people come from, what language they speak, whether they're young or old, what their gender is, or what their activity or interest might be, these simple rules have directly applied to every one of my clients. They've all recognized the validity of these simple rules in their lives and their work.
- *Infallible,* since they have yet to be proven incorrect.

Respecting the rules will allow you to shape your thinking so that you'll be able to perform to the best of your ability when called upon to do so. Adopting a mindset that violates these rules will most definitely affect your personal performance in a negative way. As a consequence, the results you achieve won't be the best that you're capable of in that situation or performance. If you make the choice to embrace a mindset that respects these rules and strive to teach the basic tenets of these rules to your children, you (and they) will be better able to develop the kind of mental control that will lead to that sought-after but elusive quality high-performance individuals often refer to as *mental toughness.* Fortunately, we don't have to understand all the intricacies of how the mind works to accomplish this goal. We just need to keep a few simple rules in mind.

CHAPTER 2

Rule #1

If You Want to Climb Out of a Hole, the Very First Thing You Must Do Is *Stop Digging!*

Have you ever found yourself in a mental "funk" and weren't really sure exactly how you got there? When you ultimately became conscious of just how bad a place you were in mentally, you wondered how your thoughts shifted to become so negative. The slippage in your thinking was gradual and insidious, and you weren't even aware that it was happening until you "woke up" somewhere down in that deep, dark, emotional hole. And the simple truth is, the deeper the mental hole we find ourselves in, the harder it is and the longer it takes to climb out of it.

Think about this rule for a moment and consider it literally. If you were in a real hole that is ten feet deep but were charged with the act of digging, it would be impossible for you to continue digging and climb out of that hole at the same time. You wouldn't be able to accomplish both actions simultaneously because they're mutually exclusive. If your eyes are fixed to the ground beneath your feet and you're flailing away with the shovel, it would not be possible to climb out of that hole at the same time. This basic rule holds true when we consider how the human mind works.

If you want to think positively and productively, the first thing you must do is stop thinking negatively and destructively. This is simply because our central processor can't be processing a "good" thought and a "bad" thought at the same moment. Sometimes we dig ourselves into a mental hole by incessantly dwelling on negative thoughts that tend to become dominant, pervasive, and overriding. This negative thinking corrupts the mindset that optimizes our ability to do our best work. These negative thoughts gain strength and power the more we process them, and before we know it, we're staring at the bottom of a hole while continuing to dig furiously. We end up so far down that hole of negative thinking that we can't seem to find our way out. What does this act of mental "digging" look and sound like?

By and large, the act of mental digging takes the form of worry; a negative film loop with its associated negative mind chatter that we constantly replay in our mind, dwelling on all the negative possibilities that might occur even before they do—in short, the "B" factors from our Performance Equation. We worry about whether we'll be good enough, whether we'll be able to achieve the results we so desperately want, and what others might think of us if we fail, and this self-doubt cripples us and corrupts our performance. This is because our focus shifts away from what we should be focused on in that moment toward the things we're worried about. How often do you catch yourself dwelling on the perceived negative consequences of some *potential* mistake that hasn't even happened yet . . . and may not ever happen? Does this internal self-recrimination influence your performance when you find yourself in such a moment of turmoil? How can it not? And our children suffer from this "digging" disease just as we do since life in general reaffirms to them that results are so incredibly important. It turns out that the fear of failure is the most pervasive fear that we all wrestle with in the moment of our performance, regardless of our age.

"Show me how to keep my confidence high, especially when things are not going well."

Figure 1: The Act of Mental Digging

The more we worry about failing and the more we focus on the outcome of what we're doing, the harder it is for us to deliver the quality of execution (in the moment) that ultimately yields the result that we're seeking. The more we doubt ourselves and focus on things that we can't control (like whether we'll win or lose or what others might think or do), the greater is our level of anxiety in that moment because our thoughts are directed not to our actions, but to the *consequences* of our actions. We shift out of the mode of doing and slip into judgment mode, processing how well or how poorly we think we're doing as we're doing it.

The real problem here is that by allowing ourselves to think negatively, we become incapable of thinking positively and in a task-focused manner at the same time, and our performance necessarily suffers. This act of digging is the basis for the loss of confidence that has become such a pervasive way of life for many people as they contemplate the many challenges that life throws in their path.

Rule #1 affirms that you must first put the shovel down if you're going to be successful in shifting your mindset from negative thinking to positive and productive thinking. To accomplish this important step, you must first become *aware* that you're thinking incorrectly (negatively) and then *choose* to actively redirect your thinking in order to process positive and productive thoughts. If you don't consciously and willfully stop the digging and put the shovel down, you won't be able to deliberately shift your dominant thought to the kind of positive and task-focused thinking you need to turn yourself around and climb out of the mental hole you've dug for yourself. This is a willful, deliberate act that you must engage purposefully because it's unlikely to just happen by itself. It requires an active control of your thoughts.

Is the secret then the power of positive thinking? Well, yes and no. Yes, in that it's far better to possess a positive mindset than a negative one, and we'll expand on this statement as we review Rule #3 of the Mental Road later in the book. But no, in that it's not good enough in a demanding, performance-centered environment to only be positive. Your thoughts must also be productive, and by productive, I specifically mean task-focused.

How do we go about respecting Rule #1 in the way we think?

The first step is to become vigilant for negative thinking, to learn to *eavesdrop* on our own internal mind chatter and "catch ourselves" as we begin to think negatively or counterproductively. It's the art of self-listening that involves paying attention to (being aware of) the little creature that sits on our shoulder and whispers in our ear—and ultimately controlling what it says! How often do we allow that little creature to whisper suggestions and thoughts that undermine our ability to perform without challenging these negative assertions? The sooner we become aware of the tone of the feedback *we give ourselves* and control it to be both positive and focused on the task in which we're engaged, the sooner we'll stop digging, put the shovel down, and begin to climb out of the hole.

This is also where we as parents and mentors can be particularly helpful as we can point out to our children when they are, in effect, digging. When they're caught up in the middle of a downward-spiraling thought process, just like us they're not always conscious that they're gradually slipping into that dark hole. Sometimes it just takes a comment from an important person to kindly and gently point out what isn't obvious to them. It's easy to see what digging looks like if you pay attention to the words they speak and the tone of their voice, and observe their body language. It's pretty clear from their behavior and their words when they're in a deep hole. Here are just a few examples that can serve to illustrate the point:

- *From a young football quarterback in high school:* "This team is so much better than we are. Look at the size of their offensive line. They're going to kill us. They're going to kill me! They're faster and stronger than we are, and we don't stand a chance. They'll surely clean our clock. Our goose is cooked!"

- *From a young competitive cyclist getting ready for a big race:* "This is a really important event toward the season-long championship, and I need to show well. But the course is tough, and there's a lot of climbing. I never do well when there are difficult climbing stages because I just don't have the fitness. Not only that, my bike is not a top-of-the-line model like the ones my opponents are riding. I don't have the kind of technical support system that they do. I'm already behind the eight ball, and there's no way I can compete with these guys. I'll give it my best, but I know that today is the day I lose the race."

- *From the shy high-school senior who's laboring over asking the girl he fancies to the prom:* "Boy, is Suzie ever hot! She's smart, one of the most popular girls in school and the top cheerleader on the team. I doubt that she'd ever be interested in going to the prom with someone like me. She'll surely end up going with one of the star football players. I don't know why I'm even contemplating asking her out because there's no way she'd even consider it. I'm not popular or good-looking. I might as well resign myself to the fact that I'll end up going to the prom without a date."

Very young children likely won't be able to intellectually (or emotionally) understand what this rule really means, but you can still help them redirect their thinking by the kind of feedback you offer when you observe that they're digging. For example, you might say, "Well, Billy, we can't control that so let's not worry about it. Instead, let's focus on this because this is something we *do* control" or "Worrying about that isn't going to help you to do your best, so just focus on your job, give your best, and just let the rest look after itself."

As your child gets older, if you take the time to explain to them in age-appropriate language the basic principle of the "digging" rule as it applies to their mindset, you can then use a simple phrase such as "You're digging, sweetie. You can't control that so don't waste your energy worrying about it. Put the shovel down" to help them redirect their thinking and change their perception regarding the situation they're wrestling with. If you remain aware and listen for mental digging on the part of your child and help them to redirect their thoughts to positive and task-focused ones—in the moment—you'll help them to learn how to execute this kind of self-coaching as they get older.

The good news is that we create our own set of mental images and thoughts in our conscious mind, and this, in turn, directly influences—through the action of our unconscious mind—our feelings, the behaviors that flow from those emotions, and our ability to perform.

Unfortunately, the bad news is that we create our own set of mental images and thoughts in our conscious mind, and this, in turn, directly influences—through the action of our unconscious mind—our feelings, the behaviors that flow from those emotions, and our ability to perform.

Rule #1 of the Rules of the Mental Road demands that we become vigilant for the wrong kind of thinking and squash it as soon as we recognize it. We then must immediately replace it with the right kind of thinking.

CHAPTER 3

Rule #2

The Mind Can Only Actively Process ONE Thought *at a Time*

Many people believe they can mentally process more than one thought at a time because they don't really understand what multitasking is all about. In fact, they can't. The reason for this is related to how the human mind processes information. Let's dig into this a little more deeply by first trying a simple experiment.

Because this test won't work well with me trying to guide you, the reader, I'd like you to try this exercise with someone else. I'll explain here what you need to do, and you can then guide them through it. Tell your subject—it could be a single person or even a group of people, it doesn't matter—that it's a simple mental-processing task that you'd like their help to investigate. It's important that they actually focus on the task you're going to ask them to undertake, so get them to relax, pay attention, and then engage in the exercise with their full attention.

Explain to the individual or group that this simple mental task consists of counting backward from one hundred by threes, out loud (as a group, if you've got a group trying this), but only when you ask them to begin. Tell them before you start the test that while they're accomplishing this task, you're going to also give them a simple mathematical problem that you want them to solve and call out the answer to you, once they've solved it. Make certain they understand you also want them to continue executing the backward-counting task as well. Their job is to process both tasks at the same time. Then tell them to begin counting backward and, when they get to ninety-one say, "Two times three equals what?" Observe what happens.

You can probably guess even before you conduct this little experiment what's going to happen, but I'll share with you what *always* happens when I do this with my clients, whether one on one or with groups in seminars, etc.

Some people are obviously better with numbers than are others as they count backward more quickly and with less difficulty. Regardless of the cognitive strategy each person utilizes to accomplish the task, you can tell that they're focused on the specific task you've given them. They call out the sequence of numbers in the correct order for the most part. Then, when you give them the simple equation "two times three" to resolve, what happens?

The first thing that happens is they hesitate as they recognize that you asked them a question. They then stop processing the task of counting backward and their internal focus of attention shifts to consider the question they heard. They evaluate the math problem you asked them to solve, quickly calculate the answer in their mind, and then give it back to you. Their internal focus of attention then shifts back to the primary task of counting backward as they seek to remember where they were and then get back to the original job at hand. Some people have difficulty shifting back because they actually start thinking about the point that the exercise is trying to get across. Before they reengage the original task, they "consult" their short-term memory to determine where they were in their counting sequence and then reengage the process with the same cognitive strategy that they'd employed at the outset. We can describe the process of what took place from a cognitive point of view with the simple flow diagram illustrated in Figure 2.

The truth is, if we could actively process two thoughts at the same time, we should be able to continue the task of counting backward *without cognitive interruption,* while at the same time undertaking the calculation of our answer to the simple mathematical problem. Would it surprise you to find out that no one on the planet can effectively process both of these very simple tasks at the same time? So what is actually going on here?

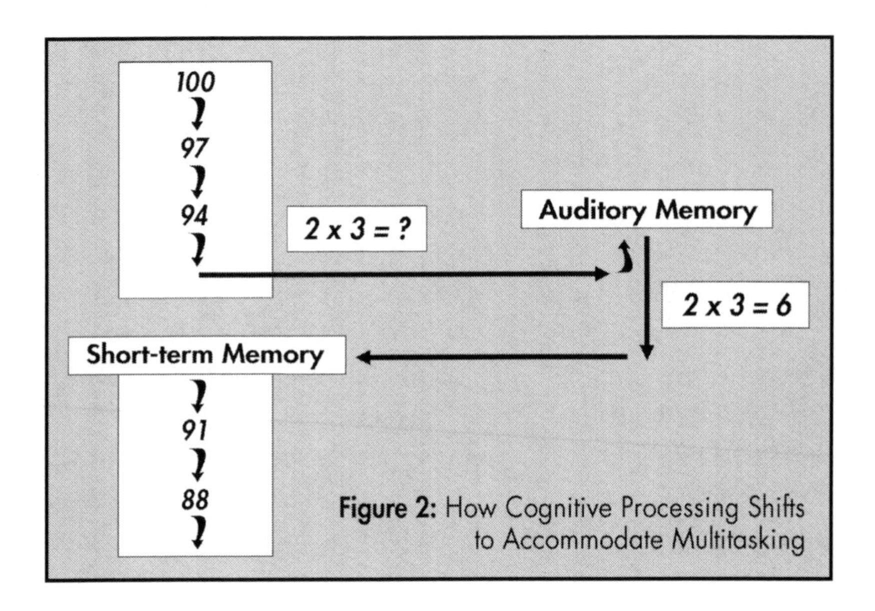

Figure 2: How Cognitive Processing Shifts to Accommodate Multitasking

While the human brain is capable of millions of computations each second, our mind can only *consciously* process this information one piece at a time. Essentially, our mind isn't capable of actively processing two thoughts at the same time! Many people believe that they can, but in practical terms, they can't; they misunderstand what multitasking is all about. What happens when we multitask is that we switch back and forth between different thoughts, albeit very quickly sometimes (in thousandths of a second), but still it's a process where we shift our internal focus of attention from one thought to another and then back again, or perhaps to a third or fourth thought if we've really got a lot of different things "on our mind."

But just like if we were trying to physically juggle too many balls at the same time—that is to say, we attempt to mentally engage too many tasks in the same timeframe—we start to make mistakes. This often leads to failure because we don't focus sufficiently on any one of them to be effective. What's the impact of Rule #2 on performance? Simply put, it's this: If your mind is only able to actively process one thought at a time, you'd better make certain that it's directed to the right thought, one that is relevant to your performance *in that moment*.

The implications of this very simple rule are significant, and this basic principle underlies the key issue that most people wrestle with on a daily basis—that of *mental focus*. This basic rule asserts that if you're focused on this (whatever "this" might happen to be), you can't be actively processing that (whatever "that" might be) at that same moment. So, is the solution simply to focus more? I certainly hear this all the time in the competitive environment: "You're not focused, Billy! You've got to focus more if you want to improve!" How often do we hear this in the classroom environment? "Tom just isn't focused. If he doesn't buckle down and focus more, he won't make it out of this class." All we have to do is focus more to do better, right?

Based on my observations over the years, focusing more *isn't* the solution, and here's why. If you're focused on the wrong thing, how does focusing more help? In reality, it doesn't. It actually makes the problem worse.

The real solution to this key performance problem is to focus *correctly* on those things that are relevant to your performance in the moment when you're called upon to perform. Fundamentally, this is why the problem we all typically face is not really one of an inability to focus, but rather it's a lack of *control* over how we *deploy* our focus of attention in the moment of our performance. Children suffer from this generally weak ability to control focus, just as we do.

We sometimes chastise them for not "paying attention," but the truth is, they *are* paying attention. The problem is that sometimes they're paying attention to something other than what we want them to, which in that moment ends up being the wrong thing. They might be daydreaming about the football game scheduled for later that evening, the dance competition that's coming up that weekend, or that cute girl in their class, rather than focusing on the material that's being presented in class. It's the same issue they often wrestle with when they're studying for an upcoming test. They might be putting in the necessary time to study but because of distractions and a scattered and constantly shifting focus, they're not very effective at consolidating and retaining the material. The challenge we face in this situation is to help them to recognize that their focus is misdirected at that moment and teach them how to take control of their focus of attention and redirect it to the right thing at the right time. This is what will actually help them to generate their best performance.

If we examine the scientific literature that deals with the area of concentration or focus, it's worth keeping in mind that four key factors strongly influence what we tend to focus on. This is of particular importance because Rule #2 affirms that we can't actively process more than one thought at a time. Here's what the research tells us:

1. *We tend to focus on things that are important to us, not on things that aren't.* This is a big one that guides everyone's focus. If we're interested in something, the activity captures our attention, and we don't generally have too much difficulty focusing on it, but if we're not interested, it's really difficult to mentally attend to it for any length of time. This helps explain why children often don't have any problem focusing for hours on a video game but struggle to keep their attention on what's going on in front of the classroom for even a short time if they're really not interested in the topic being discussed or the boring way it's being delivered. It also helps explain why many men generally have a tough time staying tuned in when women discuss the lat-

est fashion trends or why many women disengage mentally when men discuss the intricacies of play during the football game. (I'm not trying to be sexist here . . . Honest!)

So how can you use this principle to help children focus more effectively? In simple terms, you have to help your children understand how what you're asking them to do is relevant *to them*. If you're teaching history, for example, how does the material they're studying from the past inform *their lives* today? Are there parallels between then and now, for example? Give them context to understand how what they're engaged in fits into the big picture of their lives, their goals, and the lives of their families—*why* it's relevant to them. If you can engage them in this way, they will be more likely to focus effectively on what they're doing.

2. *The more challenging the task is, the more we tend to focus on it . . . but only up to a point.* When things are really easy, we don't expend much brainpower directed to the task we're engaged in, but if we perceive that the task is challenging, we tend to focus more on what we're doing. This basic principle explains why very skilled people sometimes make rookie mistakes, for example. Because they've "been there and done that" thousands of times, they don't assign much mental focus to the task in front of them, and they sometimes get caught out because they're not paying attention to what matters in the moment.

   This is an interesting one though because this holds true only to a point. If they perceive the task in front of them is totally beyond their capacity to achieve it, they mentally disengage from it and give up. The significance of this principle as it impacts children is critical because it speaks to the nature of the goals they set for themselves (and that we set for them). On the one hand, the goals must not be too low for their abilities or knowledge, or they'll disengage mentally from the task because it's too easy and doesn't challenge them. They won't feel as if they've accomplished anything and will quickly become bored and lose interest. On the other hand, their goals must be ambitious but "doable." If the bar is set too high, again, they'll mentally disengage and give up at the first sign of difficulty because they believe that there's no way they can be successful. Short-term, reasonable goals adjusted as they progress seem generally to work best.

3. *When things are routine, our focus of attention tends to "soften" because we become disinterested and then bored (see factor #1).* When our environment remains constant and things don't change much if at all, our focus of attention can sometimes drift to thoughts of other things. We don't find the environment stimulating anymore, and we have a tough time staying correctly focused. The key, of course, is to shake things up a bit sometimes (remembering that most children—and adults—are creatures of habit) in order to stimulate a renewed interest in what they're doing.

4. *Our focus of attention tends to be strongly redirected to unexpected things in our environment.* People in the world of psychology refer to this as an "orienting reflex"—a mental-processing function that has evolved in the mind of virtually every species since the dawn of time. It's saved our lives in many instances over the millennia because it caused us to turn and notice something that was unusual or unexpected in our environment, and perhaps as a result of that awareness, we were able to take some action that saved our life. It's a natural reflex response for our kids to become "distracted" by things in their environment (the puppy that walks by, the song that comes on the radio, the group of children playing nearby, the pretty girl or attractive young man who walks by, etc.). The challenge is to minimize the amount of distractions in our environment, and when distractions do occur, to recognize them as such and as quickly as possible, redirect our focus to the right thing.

With these four key factors in mind, I'd like to take a moment to briefly discuss the issue of attention deficit disorder (ADD), since it's being diagnosed in young children more and more every day. I'd also like to offer some food for thought, based on my personal experience.

As part of the training program I conduct with my high-performance clients, I undertake an initial evaluation of their cognitive (mental) skills that is both extensive and objective. This evaluation takes the form of testing over a period of eight to nine hours continuously and involves elements of concentration, timing, memory, decision-making, etc. It's a grueling process that leads the majority of these high performers to become mentally "fried"!

In a surprising number of instances, I've had clients visit with me who shared that they'd been diagnosed with ADD when they were young or even as adults. However, the vast majority of these individuals made the decision to quit taking their prescribed medications for this condition because of side effects that negatively affected their performance. While noting this fact, we forged ahead with the testing program as usual. Would it surprise you to learn that on average, these individuals did just as well as others in the high-performance database who had not been diagnosed with this condition, and many performed better than the norm for this group? How is it possible that individuals who supposedly have significant problems with focus can excel to this level in extensive, rigorous tests of concentration and other mental skills over the period of a full day without rest?

Now before you're tempted to send me irate letters decrying my insinuation that ADD is not a real condition, let me set the record straight. I do, in fact, believe that attention deficit disorder is a real condition, and some individuals afflicted with this disorder need medications to help control their condition and improve their ability to function. I just don't believe that it's nearly as prevalent as the number of diagnoses for the condition might suggest.

Instead, I believe that many children (and even many adults) simply haven't learned *how* to control their focus of attention. We tend to focus on what's of interest to us and not on what isn't, and I think that in many instances this serves as the root of the problem for people of all ages who seem to have difficulties concentrating. I think that my ADD clients generally do well in the testing phase of the program because what we're doing is of significant interest to them and they are by and large fully attentive. How much might these four factors above account for the behaviors that are interpreted as attention deficit disorder? Food for thought . . .

Because controlling focus of attention has always been so important, over the years I've used a simple analogy to get the point across to my clients. You can use this simple, practical imagery model or technique yourself to begin to more effectively exert control over how you deploy your focus of attention, and you can share this simple technique with your children as well when they're ready.

Think about concentration using the analogy of a flashlight, as illustrated in Figure 3. The flashlight I am referring to is one of those adjustable ones, where twisting the head adjusts the beam of light to be narrow or wide depending on the position you select. Consider your focus to be an adjustable beam of light (like that coming from a flashlight), where you have full control over this "beam of concentration." You can choose if the focus will be broad, directed to a wide array of objects/information in your environment (much like a floodlight would reveal), or relatively narrow and intense when focused on a specific object or idea (more like a spotlight). This "beam of concentration" can also be turned inward to consider a broad array of mental thoughts, images, and feelings or to a single thought, depending on how narrow your focus is. When your beam of concentration is broad (whether it's directed internally or externally), it takes in a lot of information from a variety of sources, but when it's directed in a narrow way, it intensifies as it's targeted to the single or few object(s) of your focus.

Conceptually, it's like adjusting the head on your flashlight to

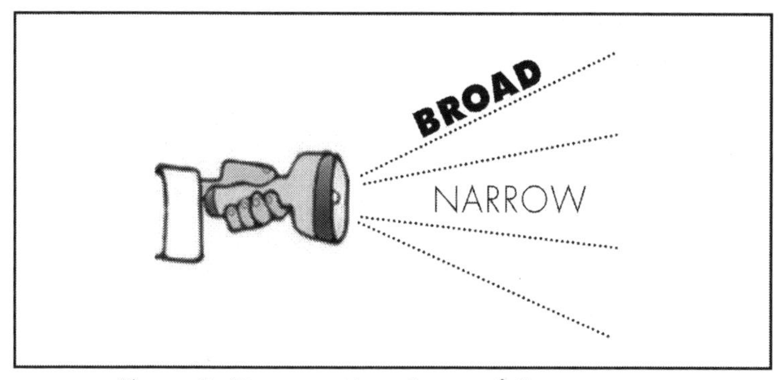

Figure 3: Directing Your Beam of Concentration

make the beam more or less narrow, and controlling its direction so that it is on the right thing at the right time. Using this simple imagery technique, you can begin to consciously become more aware of how and where your focus of attention is directed (deployed) and subsequently impose control over the direction and intensity of your "beam of concentration." With this simple tool, you can ask the question, "Where is my beam of focus directed right now?"

It should be obvious by now that it's really important to be aware of exactly how your focus is being directed. Recognize how your focus changes over time and what the right focus is for a given situation, and become more aware of when your focus is not directed correctly. In essence, you must become more effective at *eavesdropping* on your own mind chatter, and by doing so, you'll recognize when your focus of attention is inappropriate or needs to change because of the changing situation around you. The sooner you're able to do this, the better off you are from a performance point of view.

This kind of awareness is important for your children as well, and you can help them to become more attentive to the deployment of their focus of attention. Listen to their feedback, and you'll usually be able to determine what they're focused on. If you perceive that they're focused on the wrong thing, "coach" them to redirect their focus to the right thing, generally to elements of execution related to the task in front of them. Most of the time, you'll probably notice that their focus tends to be directed toward the outcome or on thoughts associated with how others might perceive them, and they often need help to shut down this natural tendency and redirect their thoughts toward what they can control.

If you think back to your own "best ever" past performances, it's likely that you would describe your mindset in those moments something like this: "I had a single-minded focus that was directed exclusively to the task in which I was involved, where my mind was fully absorbed in the process of what I was doing." This process-focused, undistracted, here-and-now mindset is a common characteristic reported by many people at the moment of their most brilliant performances, whether it's in the arts, in sport, in business, or wherever. Some people refer to it as being "in the Zone."

Now consider what kind of thinking corrupts this mindset:

- Worrying about how you're being perceived by others or fearing that you won't perform well enough to achieve your goal or to live up to someone's expectations.
- Worrying about results rather than being focused fully on the process of what you're doing—thinking about winning the game or the importance of making your monthly sales quota, etc., instead of on the actions that will lead you to these goals.

The consequence of having your mind preoccupied with processing thoughts that aren't related to your actual performance is that it makes it impossible to be focused fully on the process of execution at the same time. This is the basis of the age-old performance problem referred to as "paralysis through analysis." Sometimes you can become so preoccupied with mentally trying to "calculate" all the possible options and ramifications of your actions that you become incapable of acting to capitalize on a momentary window of opportunity. You get caught up in a whirlwind of thought associated with the many choices you have regarding what you might do and what could happen as a result of doing it.

In these situations, it's likely that your performance in whatever you're doing won't be as good as it could otherwise be. It doesn't automatically mean that you won't be successful; it just means that your personal performance won't be optimized, and your part in that performance won't be as good as it could have been. It might lead to failure, as it often does, but then again, it might not. It's important to realize that it doesn't matter whether it's a good thought or a bad thought; if it's the wrong thought, it isn't relevant to your performance in that moment, and your performance will likely suffer.

You'd probably be surprised how many successful high-performance athletes and occupational professionals have acknowledged to me over the years instances where they were very near to a significant success only to see that success evaporate in an instant because they made a fundamental error in thinking. They allowed their thoughts to *shift* away from execution as they approached their goal and started to focus on the goal or outcome itself: victory, the Olympic podium, or on counting the fruits of the victory . . . even though the event wasn't over yet! With this "end game" focus, they then made a simple error in execution because they were disengaged from what they were actually doing, and that momentary shift in focus resulted in disaster.

They gave up the task-focused mindset that put them in a position to win in the first place in favor of a goal-focused mindset that ended up costing them the game. Remember the basic truth of the "A" × "B" = Results equation because this is what we're talking about. If you're worried about and focused on the outcome or on the factors you can't control, you can't be actively processing and engaged with the actions associated with execution at the same moment. Your focus will be incorrect, and there is a greater chance you'll deliver an error in execution.

Rule #2 also helps us to understand why we sometimes feel mentally overwhelmed when we have a lot of things on our plate, and we can end up emotionally and mentally drained, confused, and unable to think straight. It's a problem that's infinitely more common than you might think, and it occurs fundamentally because of Rule #2.

Sometimes we find ourselves in situations where we have to deal with a lot of stuff (where people or circumstances are pulling us in different directions, all seemingly at the same time). We feel as though we're drowning because we have so much we have to process and we become mentally overwhelmed and somewhat discombobulated. We just can't seem to keep things straight in our mind because of all the competing thoughts and information we're trying to manage. Fundamentally, this happens because we're trying to process a multitude of things at the same time and we simply can't, because our mind can only actively process them one thought at a time. So how can we mitigate this natural tendency to become somewhat overwhelmed when faced with a lot of stuff to deal with? Here are two simple strategies that can help:

1. The first strategy involves being well organized. By being better organized, you can more effectively regulate the amount of information you have to process at any given time and, in such a way, reduce the tendency to feel overwhelmed by the need to consider too much information in a narrow window of time. If you manage your time effectively, you don't end up leaving so much to deal with at the last minute. This is certainly an argument that your child can understand if you present it consistently over time with age-appropriate language. The more well organized they are (within reason, because they are kids after all), the less they'll have to deal with at the last minute. While it won't be as bad as it might have been because they're now more organized, there may still be some overload in this situation. This is where the second strategy comes into play.

2. The second strategy involves the sorting of your choices, to prioritize the tasks that you have to deal with and then focusing on each one in turn, one at a time.

It doesn't mean that you only attend to a single task until it's completed (because this is somewhat unrealistic in the real world), but rather that you multitask in a way that allows you to focus on each task in turn. The key is to fully connect to each task when you're engaged in that task until it's appropriate to set it aside and shift your focus (willfully and purposefully) to another task.

The problem for many people is that they don't exercise this kind of control over their focus of attention but allow the environmental situation around them to define the target of their focus. And since there's a lot going on in their environment, the head seems to be on a swivel where their focus of attention is dragged back and forth, up and down, at such a rate and in so many directions that they become cross-eyed and can't think straight. This problem doesn't only occur with adults; it happens with children as well. When they're in busy environments where there's a lot being asked of them, their focus shifts all over the place and they sometimes end up highly focused . . . on the wrong things. Add to this the overwhelming availability of information that occurs because of technology, and the problem is compounded. It's important that you help them to recognize when their focus is incorrect for the situation at that moment, and then coach them to redirect their focus to the correct thing.

Rule #2 simply states that the mind can only actively process one thought at a time, and this rule demands that our focus of attention be directed to the correct thing at the correct time—the Holy Grail of the Performance Equation.

CHAPTER 4

Rule #3

You Can't *NOT* Think About Whatever Is on Your Mind

Question: The more you try to *not* think about something, what typically happens?

Answer: The more you tend to think about it.

Because your unconscious mind takes its direction from your conscious, dominant thoughts, the more you try to *not* think about something, the more the image you're trying to avoid gains strength and shape as it's conjured up in your mind's eye. By expressing things in the negative, whether you state them out loud or simply process them as internal mind chatter, you're in fact directing your thoughts to be focused on exactly what you didn't want to do, picturing the performance or its outcome in your mind's eye exactly the way you didn't want to do it. This is the fundamental problem that arises from negative thinking. Whatever thought you end up processing becomes dominant in your conscious mind, and it directs your unconscious mind to lead you to feel, behave, and perform in a way that's consistent with that dominant thought.

Here's a simple exercise that will hopefully help to drive the point home. Again, because it won't likely be as effective if you read this exercise to yourself, I encourage you try it with someone else who's close at hand. Read through the instructions first and then come back and try it out. The exercise simply requires that you ask your subject first to relax and focus on what you're going to tell them, and then give them the following instructions:

> "I DON'T want you to think about the image I'm going to describe to you in the next few moments. I DON'T want you to picture in your mind's eye:

> A HUGE PINK ELEPHANT . . . (pause)
>
> Wearing . . . PURPLE BOXER SHORTS . . . (pause)
>
> With . . . BIG YELLOW DOTS painted all over them . . ."

Pause again for a moment. Then ask them how they did and whether they ended up picturing the pink elephant with purple shorts covered in big yellow dots. It's difficult to avoid "seeing" it in our mind's eye, isn't it? Even though we understand the instruction we were given *not* to think about the elephant, in most instances, we're not able to prevent ourselves from creating that very picture in our mind. Remember, the human mind essentially thinks in pictures.

If you want to avoid seeing the image of the pink elephant in your mind's eye, you would need to rely on and utilize the principle behind Rule #2. In order to NOT see the pink elephant in our example, you'd need to direct your conscious, dominant thought to process something else, another image that grabs your attention fully (for example, that of a small orange squirrel with a long, red bushy tail). The vast majority of people who try this little exercise end up picturing that strange pink elephant in all of its glory, even when they fully understood the explicit instruction you gave them not to do so. What's the impact of Rule #3 on performance? Quite simply, it's a fact that you can't NOT think about whatever's on your conscious mind, and whatever that thought is, your unconscious mind will seek to make it happen.

So often, we mentally pre-program ourselves (as well as others around us) for failure by openly expressing things negatively. Just as important, we think about them in the negative as well, not realizing what specific impact those instructions levied by that small creature sitting on our shoulder might yield. We can't help being negatively affected by negative thinking any more than most people can't help picturing the pink elephant in our example above. Consider the mental imagery that's generated as a result of the following statements:

- "Don't get nervous. There's nothing to be nervous about. Don't worry about the audience's reaction," just before you take the stage for the big recital.
- "Go out and have fun but don't let the strikers through or we'll be in big trouble" just before you take the field for the big game.
- "This is a really important account for the company. Just do your best, but don't screw it up or the boss will be looking for someone's head!" driving your anxiety through the roof just before you step into the room to negotiate the big contract.
- "You can try if you want to, but you're wasting your time. No one is buying," creating an expectation of rejection and failure.
- "Whatever you do, don't crash the car! We don't have enough spare parts to fix it."
- "Make sure you stay out of the rough on the right side of the fairway. It's treacherous there, and if you get in the rough, you'll never be able to get out of there cleanly."
- "How many times have I told you NOT to ________________?" [fill in the blank]

As these few statements above serve to illustrate, we frequently express comments in a manner that leads others (as well as us—guided by our own internal mind chatter) to actually perform more poorly. We don't realize the consequences of our statements because we don't consider the message that the little voice in our head is actually delivering.

In these examples, the predominant image we *implant* into the mind of the receiver at the moment of their performance—by the choice of our words or description—is the very action we hope they'll avoid! We offer the directive, "Don't be nervous, afraid, or frustrated," but the very picture we implant in their mind by our statement is that of them being nervous, afraid, and frustrated . . . and the "pink elephant" materializes in their mind. As the dominant mental program at that moment, the images of incorrect execution or behavior they picture in their mind as a result of our instructions are translated into a sequence of physical actions that result in more easily achieving that very outcome. In these situations, the internal mind chatter that our input stimulates undermines the very thing that we're trying to achieve, and it's almost impossible not to suffer a breakdown in performance. Because of this, we need to become more attentive and discriminating in the phrasing of the message that we communicate—both with our children and with ourselves.

I'd like to take a small detour here to address the issue of nonverbal communication because it's critically relevant to accurately understanding the message that's being communicated to our children when we interact with them. This is especially true because of Rule #3.

Noted UCLA teacher, researcher, and author Dr. Albert Mehrabian spent a significant portion of his professional academic life studying the field of communication. (One of his key works is the highly acclaimed book *Silent Messages*.) His pioneering work shed light on the importance of nonverbal communication, and with all due apologies for oversimplifying his work, he essentially showed that in communicating *feelings* and *attitudes* specifically, the content of the message being communicated was accounted for by three key variables: the *words* that were used, the *tone* of the voice used in communicating them, and the *facial expressions/body language* associated with their use. In a nutshell, when we interact with someone and communicate a message that has to do with feelings and attitudes, the three elements that are most relevant to the receiver of that message are the words we use, the tone we use in delivering them, and the body language that accompanies that delivery.

If you sit back and think about this, it makes sense. The words are meaningful because they embody the explicit message we're communicating, but so too are the tone of voice and facial expressions that we use in that moment of communication. It might interest you to know that Dr. Mehrabian showed in his work that the distribution of importance assigned to these three variables is as follows: words (7% of the message), tone (38% of the message), and facial expressions (55% of the message). The problem we can run into is that sometimes there's a "disconnect" between the words we use and the rest of the nonverbal cues we deliver as part of the message. His work highlights the fact that when there's inconsistency between the words used and the other nonverbal cues in the communication, the receiver of the message typically believes the *nonverbal message* as opposed to the words that are spoken.

The point I'm making here is not about the actual percentages identified above, because these numbers were specific to the questions asked and to the groups used in his study. It's the principle behind the statistics that's important. His work highlights the fact that the nonverbal cues we transmit when we communicate with our children—when discussing how we feel or what we think about something they might have said or done (our attitudes)—can have a significant impact. We need to pay close attention to the tone of our voice and to our body language because they can transmit more of a "message" than our words do. Often, we labor over the words we use, but we don't even think of these other two variables much, if at all:

- You tell your child that "everything will be alright," but you deliver the message with no smile, a pinched brow, and with a look of stress on your face.
- You tell your child that you're just "happy they did their best," but you deliver the message without energy, with a downturned mouth, looking sad, reflecting how much your child let you down.
- You tell your child "B+ is a good grade in a difficult subject like algebra," but you deliver the message without enthusiasm, with rounded shoulders, and with a clear look of disappointment.

The real message you're conveying is not actually reflected in the words you offer. With this in mind, I'd like to share with you an observation that was made to me many years ago by a friend that has to do with the word "but." I've never forgotten his input, and what he told me influences the way I communicate with people to this very day.

I had used the word "but" in a sentence during our discussion, and he immediately drew my attention to the unintentional contradiction I had just made. He shared with me how he *interpreted* what I'd said. He told me that the word "but" could be thought of as an acronym that stood for the phrase "Behold the Untold Truth." He then further shared that based on his experience—looking at it from a purely psychological point of view—people generally tend not to assign any real value or belief to what comes before the "but" and only consider as truth what comes after it. At first, I wasn't sold on his point of view; however, upon further reflection, I thought there was a lot of merit to what he'd said. Let me offer some examples as food for thought:

- *"You can try if you want to, but you're wasting your time. No one is buying."* How it's often interpreted by the receiver: *"Don't waste your time. No one is buying, and if you think otherwise, you're wrong."*
- *"You're a smart kid, but you just struggle with school."* How it's often interpreted by the receiver: *"You're actually not that smart because scoring any kind of a decent grade in school seems beyond what you're capable of."*
- *"Give it your best shot, but don't expect any miracles."* How it's often interpreted by the receiver: *"You're not very good at this, and you're going to get demolished by your opposition."*
- *"Go out there and have fun, but remember, only the top three competitors move on to the finals."* How it's often interpreted by the receiver: *"We're not out here for fun. You need to win this thing or score no worse than third or we're going home empty handed."*
- *"You're a good player, but I just don't think that your skill set will mesh well with this team."* How it's often interpreted by the receiver: *"I don't think that you're a very good player, and I'm not interested in having you on the team."*
- *"Your resume looks good, but I think the company's going in a different direction."* How it's often interpreted by the receiver: *"Your resume doesn't look that great, and we're going to keep looking until we find a candidate that really interests us."*
- *"Having fun is important, but this is the last game of the season and what we do today will determine whether we make it into the playoffs."* How it's often interpreted by the receiver: *"This game is not about having fun. Nothing matters more than us winning this game and getting into the playoffs. It rests on your shoulders. Don't blow it for us."*

What we say and how we say it can have a profound effect on the way we think, behave, and ultimately, perform. If you want to optimize your own performance, or that of others you might be coaching or mentoring, it's critical that you frame the discussion—and your instructions—in a manner that clearly outlines what the correct execution entails. This doesn't mean you should never express what you don't want them to do, because they need to know what the wrong thing looks like too. It's just that you don't want to leave it there. Follow the brief cautionary note regarding the wrong performance with an expanded expression of what the *right performance* looks like and feels like when it's executed correctly.

If you're successful in implanting this dominant thought into their conscious mind, their unconscious mind is more likely to take them to that place. Their performance will likely be closer to the best they're capable of, and, other than the influence of potential "B" factors, the results they achieve will be as good as they're capable of achieving in that situation. Of course, the same applies to us.

The sad truth, unfortunately, is that we sabotage ourselves (and our children too) routinely by violating this simple rule. Because we believe that telling them what we don't want them to do will help them to avoid those very things, we regularly tend to offer input that addresses primarily what's incorrect. But when we do this, as they step into the performance, their overriding thought is often directed toward the very things we hope will not occur—for example, crashing, becoming anxious and tongue-tied, stumbling over their words and thoughts, failing and what the consequences of that failure might represent, and what others might think of them if they mess up.

Rule #3 simply affirms that the harder you try NOT to think about something, the more strength that negative thought and its associated negative images gain, becoming firmly entrenched in your mind. You must learn to phrase things (and picture them) in your mind in positive terms, describing to yourself how you want to think and feel while you successfully accomplish the task you're focused on, rather than describing to yourself what you *don't* want to do. This is why it's better to have a positive thought than a negative one, but also why that thought should be performance relevant, rather than just positive. Consider for a moment how sabotaging our instructions can be when the only thing we offer is feedback regarding what someone may have done incorrectly (even though we might try to offer it as critique) or when we direct someone just before a major performance to *not* do what we don't want them to do.

Since you can't NOT think about whatever's on your mind and because you can actively process only one thought at a time, you must ensure that the thoughts you choose to process are associated with the act of performing, picturing in your mind's eye what you want to do, how you want to do it, and how it feels when you do it exactly that way. The more that you can do this, the more likely your performance will model that mindset. This is the basis on which the A.C.T. Model process is built.

As a final thought in this chapter, I would like to address the issue of sleep or, more correctly, the inability that some people have to get restful sleep. Over the years, many of my clients and people I have spoken with have expressed having difficulty sleeping because they can't seem to quiet their mind. This is often associated with periods when they must deal with difficult challenges or just before an important competition where there's a lot at stake. Their mind races, and they simply can't fall asleep. You can look to Rule #3 both to explain why this happens and to offer a solution for how we can stop it from doing so. The solution is simple enough, although it's not easy to implement initially.

You can't *NOT* think about whatever is on your mind. In advance of the big event or competition, if you're worrying about whether you'll be successful, whether it will come to pass as you hope it will, or whether you'll achieve your goal or not, your anxiety increases as you become preoccupied with these thoughts. Even though you may recognize at the conscious level that these things are outside of your control, you continue to process these concerns. Your mind is a whirlwind of jumbled thoughts. If you keep telling yourself to not think about these things as you lay there tossing and turning, what happens? The more you get frustrated because you can't sleep, the more you tend to dig a mental hole because you think of them more and more. As long as you're digging and beating yourself up because you can't stop thinking about things you don't want to think about, the more you think about them. That preoccupation prevents your mind from quieting.

How can you use Rule #3 to help solve this common problem? As simple as it sounds, you have to exercise control over your conscious thoughts and direct them to images and thoughts that are neutral and relaxing. This is the fundamental premise of the relaxation techniques used in yoga and other forms of meditation. By focusing on the slow rhythm of your own breathing as you inhale and exhale, and the associated relaxing of your muscles, your mind is drawn away from the thoughts that are preoccupying your mind and causing you stress. This is also where the time-proven strategy of counting sheep comes into play.

If you direct your thoughts to something that has no emotional baggage or consequence (such as the counting of imaginary sheep jumping over your bed; the soft lapping of waves as they gently break onto the shore; the wind rustling through the trees; the sensation of your own breathing as it gently goes in and out, etc.), you can't NOT think about the images associated with the thoughts you're processing. And because you can only actively process one thought at a time, while you're counting sheep, you can't be processing the thoughts and images that cause you worry at the same time. These thoughts are neutral and relaxing, and because they help direct your mind to find that peaceful place, you find it easier to fall asleep. It takes mental control, but the strategy is foolproof, and with practice, you can learn to deliberately quiet your mind in a matter of a few breaths.

CHAPTER 5

Rule #4

Your *Dominant Thought* Determines Your Emotions, the Behaviors That Flow from Those Emotions, and Ultimately, Your Ability to Perform

Because we think in pictures, whatever we process in our conscious mind as our dominant thought has a direct influence on our feelings, the behaviors that result from those feelings, and ultimately on our ability to perform. I'd like to explain this statement further by asking you to vividly imagine the scene I describe in the following paragraph. Allow yourself to mentally step through this scene as if you were an active participant, fully connected to the actions being described.

Imagine that you're standing at your kitchen counter in front of the big cutting board where you chop up your fruits and vegetables. Find a sharp knife in your cutlery drawer and set it down on the edge of the cutting board. Walk over to your refrigerator and open the door. Reach down and pull open the drawer where you keep your fresh fruit. Pick up the largest, plumpest lemon you can find in the drawer and squeeze it gently, feeling just how ripe and juicy it is. Stand up, close the drawer and the refrigerator door and walk back over to the cutting board. Put the lemon down on the board and pick up the sharp knife. Being careful to keep your fingers away from the sharp blade, slice through the lemon with a smooth stroke, cutting it in half. Smell the tart, citrusy smell that a freshly cut lemon produces. Take the knife and take one of the halves and cut it into two quarters. Put your knife down on the cutting board and take one of the quarters into your right hand. Bring it up to your face and inhale its tart fragrance. Bring the quarter of that plump, juicy lemon up to your mouth, put it into your mouth and bite down on it hard, sucking the tart, bitter juice into your mouth and down your throat. . . .

How does that feel? Did you begin to salivate as your mind played through the mental images I described above? Did your face scrunch up a little bit and your jaw tighten as you imagined biting down and sucking on the sour lemon? The vast majority of people do. This little exercise highlights one of the basic truths about how the human mind works:

The human mind doesn't differentiate between what is real and what is vividly imagined!

How else could you explain that just imagining the scene with the lemon above can cause the salivary glands in your mouth to explode and your jaw to clench at the mere thought of biting into that sour lemon? It's a revealing glimpse into how thoughts, framed as images in your conscious mind, can set into motion—via your unconscious mind—a complex series of physiological responses that leads you to engage a number of facial muscles and stimulate the production of saliva, just as though you had really bitten into that sour lemon. Not only is it interesting to recognize how effective this can be, but it can also provide insight into how we might use this basic truth to our advantage, rather than use it to sabotage ourselves.

People invariably think in pictures. In fact, there isn't a single thought we create in our mind that isn't somehow associated with a mental image of some sort—and often, with a set of associated feelings as well. We often talk about *seeing with our "mind's eye."* This simply means that when we imagine something in our mind, we generally see a picture of what we're thinking about, just as if we were looking at it through a camera lens or through our own eyes. Try thinking about something without "seeing it" in your mind's eye—your car, your desk at work, your favorite hat, and so on.

If you consider the scientific research behind imagery, it's not so hard to believe that when we vividly imagine ourselves feeling or performing in a certain way, our body automatically adjusts to act on that information. For example, when we watch a frightening movie, our heart begins to race, our muscles become tense, and our breathing speeds up or we hold our breath. When we watch a hilarious comedy, we laugh and our mood brightens. When we watch a sad movie, we become sad and may even cry. The events taking place before us aren't real since they're being played out on a movie screen by actors following defined scripts, and yet, when we imagine ourselves in these different scenarios by viewing them on a screen, our body and mind behaves in much the same way as it would if we were truly there, albeit at a lower level of intensity.

But how and why does this occur? Understanding the "why" of this process depends upon understanding the basic difference that exists between your conscious and unconscious mind. The conscious part of your mind is the rational, objective, discriminating faculty of the brain. Its role is to take in information from your environment, compare it with your previous experiences and knowledge, determine whether it's relevant or not, and then finally make a decision. But once that decision is made, every single piece of information your conscious mind accepts is then accepted by your unconscious mind as well. It's accepted as being true, as fact, even though it may or *may not* reflect reality accurately. In other words, your unconscious mind doesn't dispute the accuracy or validity of the information you process within your conscious mind; it accepts it without debate as being fundamentally true, acts accordingly, and what's even more significant, *you can't directly control it.*

If I command you right now to be happy, can you do it? Or if I ask you to be sad at this very moment, would you be able to? Obviously, you couldn't because you can't directly control your emotions any more than I can. They evolve as a result of the thoughts we process in our conscious mind. The way to feel true happiness is to consciously think "happy thoughts," and the more vividly we process those happy thoughts in our conscious mind, the more a happy or joyous mindset evolves within us. Likewise, the way to feel deep sadness is to think sad thoughts in our conscious mind, and if we're able to do so with conviction, we gradually become sadder and sadder and ultimately may become overwhelmed with sorrow. Our conscious mind is like the captain of the ship that sets the direction. Our unconscious mind then seeks to implement that direction, to act like the crew and follow the captain's orders, without debate or reservation. What I've described here is a fact of science that is defined by how our mind processes information. But how does it actually work?

In essence, images and feelings that are created in your mind activate your nervous system in much the same way that it's activated when you're experiencing the actual event. It's almost like a mind-body rehearsal for the activity that's about to occur.

I'm going to suggest an exercise in the following paragraphs that I hope will be effective in demonstrating in a practical way how mental imagery translates directly into physiological response and action. I'd like to take a moment beforehand, however, to put this task into context.

When I undertake this exercise with my clients in person or with groups of people in a live setting such as a seminar or workshop, approximately 85–90% of the participants typically demonstrate the response that's expected. For the 10–15% of participants who don't see the expected response, it's almost always associated with one of two reasons:

- First and most commonly, they misunderstand my initial instructions and believe that they're supposed to prevent the pendulum from moving; regardless of the instructions I might subsequently give (you'll understand what pendulum I'm referring to in just a few moments). When I tell them initially that I don't want them to consciously move the pendulum, they incorrectly interpret this statement as a directive to keep the pendulum still and prevent it from moving. If their dominant thought is to keep the pendulum still, the pendulum usually remains still.

- Second, individuals who tend to demonstrate an unusually tight control over their emotions generally don't give themselves over very easily to the imagery that I might describe. They resist the influence of the suggested imagery, and again, the pendulum doesn't move very much, if at all.

With this in mind, I'm not certain if this exercise will work as well in this format (that is, self-directed from a book) as it does when I undertake it in person, but I encourage you to try it nonetheless and see where it leads. You may even want to try it with another person, where you give the instructions and observe the response as executed by them or, in turn, have them read the instructions out loud to you so that you can focus on the imagery associated with the exercise. The outcome of this exercise invariably becomes an eye-opening—if not a little spooky—experience that has allowed many people to "connect the dots" and gain greater clarity on how the way they think directly influences how they perform. For many, they describe it as a significant "ah-ha!" moment that allows them to put into context many past experiences in their life. Let's turn our attention now to the specific exercise that I'm referring to with the pendulum.

As you work through this exercise, I don't want you to try to move the pendulum on purpose. If movement does start to occur, however, *allow it to move freely.* The object of the exercise is not to keep the pendulum still, nor is it to move it on purpose. It's simply to see what impact powerful imagery can have on the way our body responds to such mental images.

Start by examining the illustration presented in Figure 4. As shown in the illustration, draw two intersecting lines on a piece of paper and number each side. Then take a light string or a thin chain about 12 inches (30 cm) long and tie a metal nut or washer, a heavy paper clip, or a fishing weight to one end of it to make the pendulum. Grasp the other end of the string between the thumb and forefinger of your dominant hand, with the elbow of that arm making contact with and resting comfortably on the table. Center the hanging pendulum and suspend it just above the intersection of the two lines.

With your eyes open and focused on the pendulum, I want you to *imagine* that there's a powerful cone-shaped magnet positioned under the table, directly below the point of intersection. Picture the magnet and its magnetic effect as vividly as you can. This magnet exerts such force on the pendulum that it keeps it *perfectly still*, pulling on it right through the table at the point where the two lines intersect. The image of the pendulum being perfectly still is crystal clear in your mind's eye.

Now, imagine that the magnet is withdrawn from its position

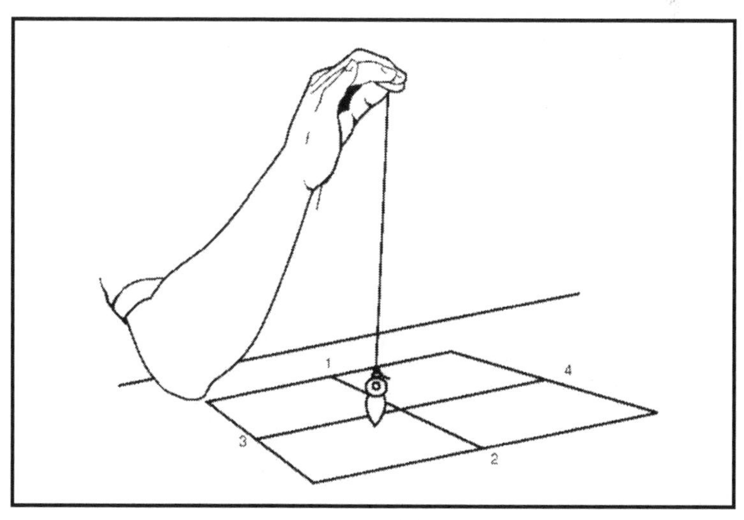

Figure 4: The Pendulum Exercise

beneath the table where the two lines cross. Then, picture in your mind's eye what the pendulum would look like if it started to ever so slowly *swing from side to side,* beginning to move gently between the numbers 3 and 4 (vividly imagine it happening in your mind's eye; see it in your imagination and feel it).

Continue to *vividly imagine* what the pendulum would look like as it *gains momentum, increasing* its side-to-side movement more and more. Still in your mind's eye, imagine the pendulum continuing to swing back and forth—moving with such amplitude and momentum that it begins to reach out toward the edges of the page with each passing swing. See the pendulum moving in your mind's eye . . . and imagine what it would *feel* like if it responded the way you imagine it, according to the clear, vivid picture in your mind of it swinging back and forth.

Now, imagine that the magnet was reinserted just below the intersection of the two lines to yet again exert its influence on the head of the pendulum. Picture the pendulum slowing down, being pulled back to the center of the two intersecting lines because of the powerful attraction of the magnet . . . through the table . . . to the center position. Imagine how it would *feel* if the pendulum were to slow down, reducing its travel, diminishing its movement, until it came to rest quietly right over the intersection of the two lines . . . the magnet pulling on it so powerfully that you must keep a firm grip on the string or it might slip through your fingers . . . perfectly still, with no movement whatsoever.

With practice and a relaxed "touch," most individuals are able to experience movement of the pendulum as they begin to imagine it moving, and then a quieting of the pendulum as they imagine the placement of the magnet with its stabilizing effect. With mental training, this ability gets stronger and you can make the pendulum move in whatever direction you imagine, simply by vividly focusing your mind on the *images* and *feelings* of the action you wish to see occur. But why does the pendulum typically move in this manner?

It's a scientific fact that your brain is constantly transmitting electrical impulses to your muscles when you execute any physical action, and we know that this kind of mental activity is even occurring at rest. We refer to the activation of muscle at rest as *muscle tone,* and it's a property of muscle cells that's universal in all species, not just humans. It's also a fact that the same electrical impulses are also being transmitted down the nerves to your muscles when you just *think* about executing the action, although the signals are sent at a lower level of intensity.

In fact, if we placed small recording electrodes for muscle activity on the muscles of your shoulder, upper arm, and your forearm, we would see the same sequence of electrical signals directed to the same motor units, whether you're consciously and deliberately controlling the movement of your arm to slowly swing the pendulum in the desired way or simply thinking about moving it. The difference lies in the intensity of the signals and not where they're directed. When you're just thinking about or imagining it, the same muscle groups are being activated, but it's like the "volume" is turned down. It's not a conscious directive to move the pendulum that occurs as you engage this exercise; it's an unconscious response to the dominant images in your conscious mind that paint the picture of the pendulum moving as you vividly imagine it.

The images and thoughts you create in your mind during the exercise with the pendulum are transferred as electrical signals to the muscles of the hand, arm, shoulder, etc., but at a reduced intensity. Imagery is kind of like using an electrical *dimmer switch* in your brain—like the ones you might have in your house to adjust the intensity of a light—in order to turn down the intensity of the electrical signals that are being sent to your muscles. As strange as it may sound, simply by imagining the movement of the pendulum in this example, you create a set of mental impulses or commands in your brain that are transmitted down the nerves to the muscles that cause the movement of your arm, but you're not consciously aware of it because it's mediated by (controlled by) your unconscious mind.

This is the same mechanism that explains why imagining that we are biting into a lemon causes us to salivate, why thinking sad thoughts often causes us to cry, why worrying about slicing into the rough on the golf course often leads to the perfect slice, and why watching a scary movie causes our heart to race and our muscles to become tense. Consider the significance of this fact for a moment—how thoughts you formulate in your mind actually trigger very real physical responses in your body as a direct consequence of what you're thinking.

How might this simple rule express itself in the real world? Consider this scenario:

Your daughter is playing on a softball team that has made it to the finals of a big regional tournament. She's recognized as the best player on the team and has been playing well coming into the final game, leading her team in hits and runs. They're in the final inning with the last at bat and a runner on base, but trailing by one run. The count is two strikes and three balls. Her performance in this moment will determine whether the game is tied, won, or lost. How might the mindset she adopts in this situation (her dominant thought) affect her performance?

If she remains calm and confident in her abilities, her focus will be fully directed to the pitcher and the throw she's about to make. Her shoulders will be loose and her balance perfect. Time may seem to slow down and her vision will be clearer than ever. She may even be able to see the strings on the ball as it's flying toward her. There will be no doubt in her mind about what she needs to do. . . .

If she's anxious because she realizes that the fate of the team rests in her hands and she's worried that she may strike out, she'll tense up. Her mental focus will be split between the pitcher and the fear of failing her team and her family. She'll be a half step behind the pitch.

Rule #4 simply affirms that our dominant thought (mindset) directly affects our ability to perform. Each of us, regardless of our age, has frequently experienced the consequences of this powerful rule in the real world. Consider the following:

- Circumstances or beliefs that lead us to become afraid, to develop feelings of anxiety with its associated physical tension, often deny us the ability to focus effectively on the task in front of us because we're focused on the things that are causing us to worry, and our performance isn't as good as it might have been.
- Situations where we feel a high degree of motivation and desire seem to allow us unlimited reserves of energy and strength.
- A loss of confidence creates periods of self-doubt where images of failure become self-fulfilling prophesies that infect and poison our feelings, behaviors, and ultimately, our performance.
- Environments that allow us to remain calm and focused usually allow us to generate and deliver our best personal performances.

Each one of us acts, feels, and behaves in a way that's consistent with our own self-image, regardless of the accuracy or inaccuracy of that image. We act and feel not according to how things really are, but according to the image our mind holds of what they're like. The truth is that we acquire our self-image through unconscious habit, shaped in part by the people around us. While it's not *easy* to change such a habit, it's *simple* enough. It just takes repeated practice implementing a new, hopefully better habit.

Just like us adults, our children believe what they hold in their mind as their dominant thought, and that mindset directly influences their emotions, their behaviors, and ultimately, their ability to perform. At the core, their self-esteem (the reputation they establish with themselves) is defined by the beliefs that are manifested as their dominant thought, and the mindset they adopt as they move through life sets the stage for moments of virtuosity or self-sabotage. Our most important job as adults is to try to influence the dominant thought of our children to create and sustain the mindset that leads them to virtuosity and to greater happiness, and to give them the tools to successfully dispute the negative dominant thoughts that we all wrestle with.

Positive and productive dominant thoughts generally preface our best performances, while negative and counterproductive dominant thoughts lead to anxiety, loss of appropriate focus, and poor performance. We can use this fundamental truth about the human mind to help ourselves perform to the best of our ability rather than sabotage ourselves through negative thinking that draws our focus away from the task in front of us. We can also use this truth to help shape the dominant mindset that our children adopt as they face the challenges that their life will undoubtedly present. This truth serves as the basis of the A.C.T. Model process that we'll discuss in Part Two of this book.

CHAPTER 6

Rule #5

You *ARE in Control* of Your Dominant Thought

There are so many things in life over which we have little or no control, but we can learn to have greater and greater control over how we see these things.

Many people don't really understand that we *choose* what we believe. Each of our beliefs is a choice that we've made at some point in our life. We then tend to allow in only information that conforms to our innermost beliefs (whether these beliefs are consistent with reality or not) and to reject information that doesn't conform to those fundamental beliefs. The most damaging effect on you and your performance comes from beliefs that you hold strongly that speak to your inability to successfully engage and accomplish the challenges you choose to take on. These self-limiting beliefs then naturally and automatically lead to self-limiting behaviors because your unconscious mind takes over. Your focus shifts away from the task in front of you to the worries you have, and then the pendulum moves. The fundamental problem we all wrestle with is relatively simple to understand, but the solution isn't quite so easy to implement because it starts with the ability to control your own mind.

If you learn how to control your dominant thought so that your mind consistently sees what it is that you want as you engage the task—and what you want to be like when you perform to the best of your ability—your personal performance will be the best that it can be given the skills, knowledge, and abilities you possess at that moment in time. Your abilities will be applied fully to the task you're focused on, and you'll deny your central processor the capacity and the opportunity to create the self-sabotaging mindset that so often infects your performance in those moments when you face your greatest challenges. You can't control outcome, but with the right kind of thinking, you can ensure that you bring your "A" Game to the performance, whatever it is that you're doing. With this mindset, you'll leave nothing on the table . . . and more than this you cannot do.

The problem is that we sometimes fail to recognize that we have 100% control over how we choose to see things in the first place, and then secondly, we systematically fail to exercise that control. So often, we allow the environment around us and the situations and challenges we face to dictate our dominant thought. We "bounce" off our environmental circumstances, and our dominant thought ends up being defined within those events, rather than by us exercising control over our mind as we face those events. Furthermore, when we feel like we're out of control, anxiety spikes and it negatively affects our performance. Our children are no different than we are in this regard.

When they face a challenging situation where they get emotionally caught up in the negatives and become fixated on things they can't control, you can coach them to dispute this negative perspective and see the situation in a different way. As you teach your child to control their dominant thought, you'll effectively teach them how to choose the tint of the filter through which they interpret the challenges and opportunities of their life. In this way, they'll become the *boss* of their own mind, and if they do so in a conscious and systematic way, they'll learn to establish a mindset that allows them to more consistently deliver their best performances on command. They'll more easily redirect their thoughts to the performance-relevant things they can control. The rub, of course, is in knowing how to do it and the A.C.T. Model process will provide you (and them) with a defined starting point to accomplish this very task.

CHAPTER 7

Rule #6

Your *Perception* or *Perspective* Regarding the Challenges You Face Will Determine Your Dominant Thought

In the 1950s, Dr. Albert Ellis, a world-renowned clinical psychologist and author, created a model of cognitive behavioral therapy that became known as "Rational Emotive Behavior Therapy." The basic tenet of this form of therapy hinges on the understanding that whenever we become upset or stressed out, it's not the events taking place in our life at that time that are causing the stress, but rather, our stress response is a direct result of the belief we hold with respect to those events. To put it another way, it's not the events in our life that cause us stress, it's our perception or interpretation of those events that leads to a stress response that, on the one hand, can be negative and counterproductive for our health and performance or, on the other hand, can be positive and contribute to our ability to perform. Dr. Ellis framed this relationship by developing a simple A-B-C paradigm where "A" leads to "B," which then leads to "C." In the paradigm, he outlined, "A" never leads to "C" directly; it *always* goes through "B":

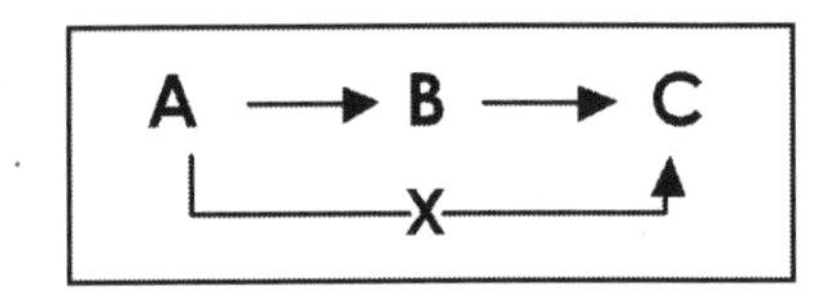

A—The *Activating* event: the situation or event that we're reacting to; often, this event is outside our direct control since it may be imposed on us by others or by circumstances in our environment . . . the "B" factors in the Performance Equation that often arise in life.

B—Our *Belief* with respect to that event: something that's fully within our control to change or adapt, assuming of course that we choose to exercise that control.

C—The *Consequences* of that belief: something that's outside of our direct control since these consequences—our emotions—are automatically defined by our unconscious mind in response to our conscious thoughts and beliefs.

Consider this concrete example that comes from the world of student life to illustrate this point:

Two seniors have decided to submit their names for president of the student council. Their candidacy, along with other school business, is supposed to be announced by the principal at the monthly school assembly. Ten minutes prior to the start of assembly, the principal informs the candidates that because other business is light this month, they will each have five minutes to address the student body to officially launch their election campaign.

Student #1 thinks to herself: *Good grief, what am I going to do? I've only got five minutes to get my election platform across to the other students. I'll never be able to convince them that I'm their best choice in that short a time. I'm not ready! I never do well in these kinds of high-pressure situations when I haven't been able to practice my speech. I get so nervous that I trip over my tongue every time! I just can't seem to get comfortable. Why did the principal ask us to present now? What if it ends up being a disaster? I could very well lose the election right here today!*

When faced with the same information, Student #2 thinks to herself: *Good grief, what a great opportunity! It's tough to get all of the students to focus on one thing at the same time, and I have them all in the same room listening to me for five minutes. I know they won't expect to get all the details of my election platform in that short a time. My job is to highlight only a couple of items and let them get to know me a little bit better. This way, when I speak with them later on they'll know where I'm coming from. I always do well when the challenge in front of me is well defined! My schoolmates put their pants on one leg at a time just like I do, and I know I can deliver the goods. What a lucky break! I can't wait to get up there and show them what I can do as student council president to help make the school better for everyone!*

Assuming that both students are equally competent and popular, it should be obvious which one is going to be more effective in their presentation and more likely to bring home the vote. Let's go back to our A-B-C explanation to put this situation in perspective.

The activating event—the "A" in this scenario—is the same for both students: Ten minutes prior to assembly, each is informed by the principal that they will have five minutes to address the student body and officially launch their election campaign.

Their belief about the event—the "B" in the perception paradigm—is quite different, however. Student #1 sees the assembly presentation as an unexpected negative, with the potential for failure! She imagines it with dread, unfolding in a disastrous way. Student #2, on the other hand, sees the presentation as a positive, an opportunity that can work to her advantage because it will allow her to be the focal point in the school for five minutes.

What are the consequences—the "C" in our paradigm—that each will realize as a result of their beliefs about this event? Student #1 is more likely to become anxious and physically tense as the presentation approaches, and the increased tension will cause her to narrow her focus and lose the mental flexibility needed to think on her feet. She'll likely be overly concerned with the consequences of a "presentation gone wrong," and she may very well become tongue-tied, just the way she imagined it in her mind. Her anxiety and lack of confidence will be observed by the others in the room, and they'll begin to question whether this individual might really be a good leader for the student council. Student #2, on the other hand, becomes energized by the thought of hitting a home run and steps up to the microphone more relaxed, confident, and mentally sharp. She'll likely be more effective at delivering a clear overview of her plans for the student council, and her easy and professional manner will have a positive impact on her audience.

I could use many more examples to illustrate this point, but I'm confident you can think of many examples in your own life where this basic rule has held true. What's the impact of Rule #6 on performance? It's simply this: Realize that in our A-B-C paradigm, "A" always leads to "B," which then always leads to "C." The activating event does *not* lead directly to the consequences. It's always our beliefs or perception regarding the events in our life that lead to the thoughts and ultimately the consequences we experience.

The beauty—and power—of this realization is that if you change your belief about the activating events in your life, you'll change the consequences you experience *because your unconscious mind will accept this new perception as being real and true, and set the direction for its actions.* This is something that is 100% within your control since Rule #5 states that "we *are* in control of our dominant thought." It's simple enough to understand as a conceptual framework; it just isn't very easy to apply consistently in the real world.

What I would like to do now is shift our discussion to touch on some additional background information I believe is important to consider that relates directly to this issue of perspective. The information I would like to focus on now deals with several important topics:

- Stress and our ability to cope with it.
- Anxiety and its influence on performance.
- The relationship between anxiety, confidence, and focus.

I suspect that these are critical issues for you, and I believe that they are equally critical issues for your children since stress is an integral part of life for all of us. And with so many distractions and pressures to succeed today, it appears that stress is at an all-time high. This information will provide context to help you to better understand where Rule #6 comes from and the power that this simple rule can have in your life. While it may represent a different way of looking at things, I hope you'll be open to considering a different perspective regarding what actually causes stress and your ability to more effectively deal with it. As you begin to better understand this issue of stress and where it comes from, you'll be in a better position to help your child cope with it more effectively.

To begin this discussion, I would like you to consider the following statements and place a pencil mark across the line between the two boxes that identifies where you believe you fall with respect to the thoughts identified in each statement. A mark closer to the **MAX** end of the line means you agree completely with the particular statement and a mark closer to the **MIN** end of the line means you do not agree at all with the statement as it relates to your life and your situation. There are no correct or incorrect answers here, so just be honest with yourself and provide the best estimate you can regarding your feelings with respect to your specific situation and beliefs.

To what degree do you feel you have personal control over your own thoughts, emotions, and behaviors, as well as over the activities in which you engage? How well do you feel you're the "boss" of your own mind?

To what degree do you feel you're an important part of your work and life interactions, enjoying the activities you're involved with and fully engaged in them? How committed are you to the path you're walking in your life at this moment?

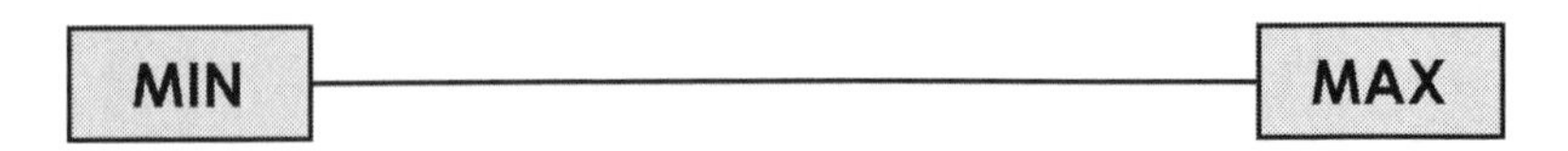

To what degree do you generally view changes in your life (whether you judge these changes to be positive or negative at the time) as a positive challenge or opportunity? To what extent do you see new situations as opportunities to grow and measure yourself against that challenge?

What degree of emotional and mental support do you feel you have with respect to problems or difficulties you may confront in your life (both in work and in your personal life)? This statement reflects the human/emotional connections you feel you can count on for support when the situation you're facing becomes difficult or challenging.

We'll come back to this exercise a little later on in this chapter as we discuss the issue of how we cope with stress.

It's safe to say that humans are creatures of habit. We tend to be comfortable with routine and, for the most part, don't manage change very well. In fact, the vast majority of people (perhaps this is even more so for young children) find change to be inherently stressful, and the more change we have going on in our life, the more stress we seem to feel. Consider the need for young children to have a relatively fixed bedtime and bedtime preparation routine, and how much changing this routine—during periods of travel, for example—can be overwhelming for them. Over the years, researchers have sought to understand how change itself is associated with health. Many clinicians have observed that the more a patient reflects a family history of ongoing significant upheaval (that is, change) in their life, the more the individual seems to wrestle with significant health issues. Intuitively, I suspect that this makes sense to most of us.

In an attempt to study this relationship more fully, in 1967 two psychiatrists, Thomas Holmes and Richard Rahe, created a questionnaire that sought to quantify how much change was going on in a person's life and studied whether the amount of change people were dealing with was, or was not, related to their health status. They essentially compared the responses from more than 5,000 patients on their "Social Readjustment Rating Scale" (which has also commonly been called the "Life Change Events Scale") against their medical history to determine the nature of the relationship between these two variables.

What they found was that, in general, the amount of change a person was dealing with in their life—as a *cumulative* variable—seems to have a direct effect on their health status. The greater the amount of life change the individual was wrestling with, the greater was the potential negative impact on their health. There was a strong statistical relationship established between "life change events" and negative health consequences, and if you look at the two black rectangles in Figure 5, you can think of them as movable sliders that seem to be tied together. This is based simply on the proven relationship that exists between life change and health. Note that the levels used in these figures are for illustration purposes only.

What this work effectively says is that the more "stuff" we have going on in our life, the greater the potential exists for negative health consequences. Interestingly, it doesn't mean that the change in question is necessarily always negative since the Holmes/Rahe Social Readjustment Rating Scale lists a number of change events that most individuals would consider positive. For example: marriage, the birth of a child, beginning school, outstanding personal achievement, going on vacation, or experiencing major holidays like Christmas. These are events in a person's life that, while positive, can still be stressful because they represent a meaningful change in the status quo and the routine of life. Anyone who has experienced the birth of a child will readily understand this perspective.

On the flip side, when there's not a lot of change going on in

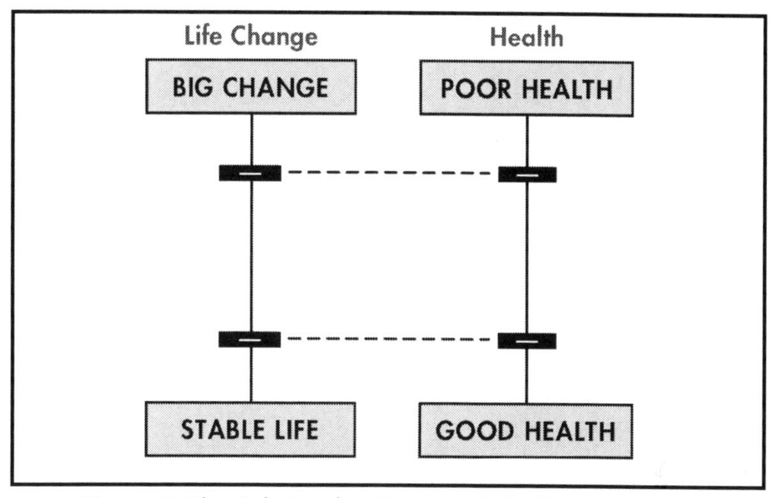

Figure 5: The Relationship Between Life Change Events and Health Status

our life, the research suggests that this more stable life situation bodes well for good health. In short, the higher the aggregate score on the Holmes/Rahe scale was, the greater was the risk for negative health consequences, while the lower the aggregate score on the scale, the less there appeared to be a risk of illness. While the data may seem to suggest that this relationship is straightforward, the situation isn't actually this simple.

The fundamental issue we're discussing here revolves around the mental state of negative arousal that we call stress. The health consequences that each of us experiences are generally accepted as being related to the level of negative stress we feel. It's well recognized today that the hypothalamus-pituitary-adrenal interaction in the brain responds to stress by releasing high concentrations of a hormone called cortisol into our body. Prolonged exposure to stressful circumstances can produce long-lasting effects on physical and mental health and, given our specific interest, on performance as well because of the long-term impact of cortisol on the body systems. The relationship between psychological stress and health is undeniable and exists as a "solid line" relationship. So the picture evolves to take on a slightly different look, as is outlined in Figure 6.

To understand this relationship more fully, however, we need to introduce into our thinking an intervening variable in the life change–health relationship that helps to explain why change (both positive and negative) seems to be so tightly related to health status. The equation again appears simple enough: A large amount of life change is normally associated, for most people, with a high degree of stress, which in turn influences the body systems to facilitate the development of illness. Intuitively, I don't think that many of us would disagree with this logic. But, again, the situation isn't really that straightforward.

Why is it that some people who are exposed to significant life-change events "crumble" emotionally and physically and the stress often associated with events such as a battle with a major disease causes them to succumb, while others don't? What is it that differentiates individuals such that some people seem to be more stress-susceptible while others seem to be stress-resistant? Researchers often refer to this kind of person as being "stress hardy" or "stress resilient."

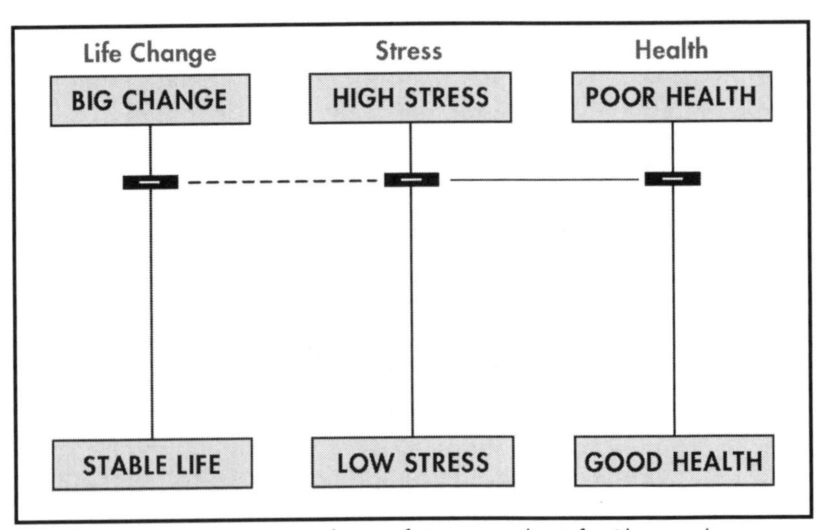

Figure 6: The Intermediary of Stress in the Life Change/ Health Equation

If we examine the extensive pool of research that seeks to understand the fundamental difference between the stress-resistant and stress-susceptible individual, it seems that the explanation lies in large part in their ability to more effectively "cope" with the stressful situations they're dealing with.

Stated another way, there seems to be an inverse relationship between coping skills and negative stress such that, when coping skills are strong, the negative stress response is muted, but when coping skills are weak, negative stress tends to be greater. We now must introduce the variable of *coping ability* into our illustration to get the full picture. Coping skills (or lack thereof) seem to account for much of the difference between stress-susceptible and stress-resistant individuals, and when coping skills are poor, especially when there are big life changes afoot, the elevated negative stress response often leads to health problems (as illustrated in Figure 7).

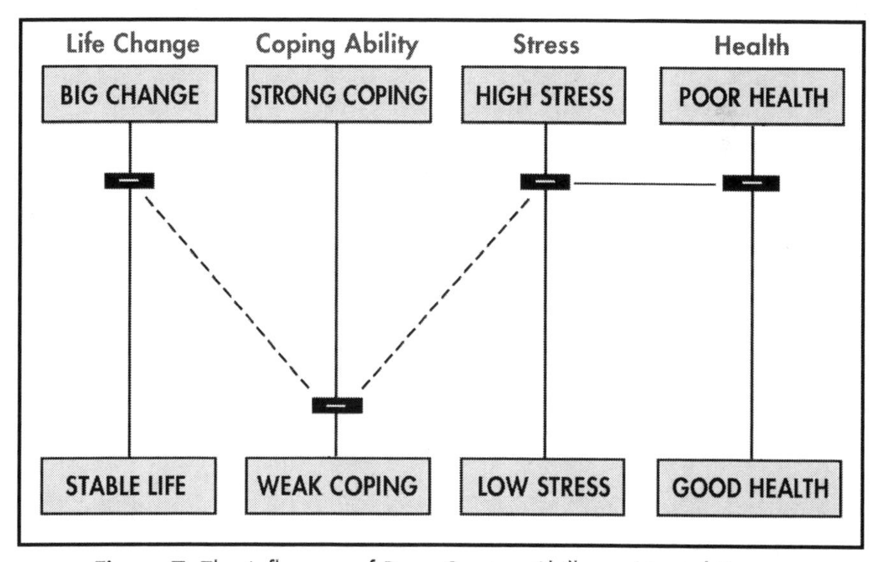

Figure 7: The Influence of Poor Coping Skills on Mental Stress and Health Status

When coping skills are weak but there aren't a lot of life changes to deal with, the stress response tends to be low as well because we're not called upon to adapt to or cope with much of anything. But when life change events spike, as they always do since one of the greatest constants in life is that things will change, poor coping skills don't allow the stress-susceptible individual much protection.

On the other hand, when the stress-resistant individual encounters a great deal of life change, their ability to effectively cope with the upheaval that those events bring yields a lower negative stress response. As we might expect, they also seem to have a lower risk of illness in these situations (as outlined in Figure 8). This simple explanation ties together a number of key components: the pressures that life throws at us, how we mentally cope with them, the stress response that is subsequently generated within us, and the effect of that stress response on both our health and performance. Since our ability to cope with stress seems to be a critical variable in this mix, let's now consider what defines our ability to effectively cope with stress.

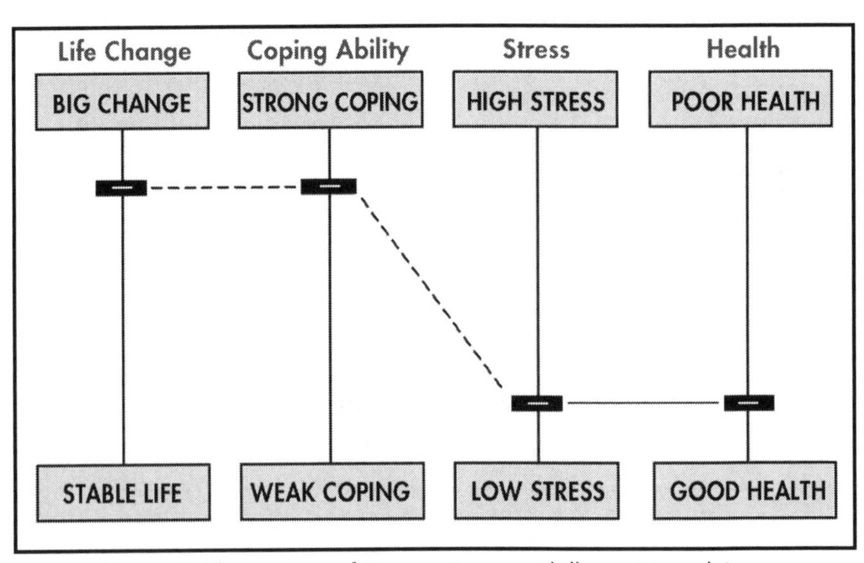

Figure 8: The Impact of Strong Coping Skills on Mental Stress and Health Status

The extensive research in this area conducted over many years suggests that the core of our coping skills can be described using four simple variables, not unlike the legs of a stool. Our coping skills (the seat of our metaphorical stool) seem to be supported by four key variables (or legs): our sense of *control;* our level of *commitment;* how we view *change;* and the level of emotional *connections* or support that we feel we have from important people in our life.

I would now like to refer back to the exercise that I asked you to complete earlier in this chapter where you placed a pencil mark across the line to describe how you felt about the statements associated with each line. In a nutshell, the more to the right you placed your mark on each line, the more that mark signals a tendency to be stress-resistant, whereas the more to the left you placed your mark, the more stress-susceptible you would tend to be. I will reproduce each statement again to make it easier to discuss them in turn:

SENSE OF CONTROL

To what degree do you feel you have personal control over your own thoughts, emotions, and behaviors, as well as over the activities in which you engage? How well do you feel you're the "boss" of your own mind?

The vast body of research essentially tells us that individuals who understand they can't control what they can't control (the "B" factors in life), but who recognize that they *have full control* over how they choose to see those events, are automatically more stress-resistant than those who have the opposite perspective.

The stress-resistant individual feels they are in control of their own thoughts and, to a large degree, are the masters of their own destiny. Their sense of control allows them to more calmly and systematically engage the challenges in front of them, and as a result, they tend to focus more on their actions rather than on the consequences of failure. Individuals who put their mark toward the left side of the line tend to feel more out of control. They perceive themselves as victims with little sense of control over their own destiny. They are a caboose on the freight train of life, which is dragging them along with no perceived sense of meaningful, personal control.

The research tells us that individuals who tend to feel victimized are more stress-susceptible. They tend to focus most of their emotional energy and thoughts on their failure to control things (which they actually can't control for the most part) and on the negative situation that they're in (the "woe is me" mindset I described previously when discussing the children of helicopter parents). They stare at their shoes, digging madly, all the while worrying about whether they will ever get out of the mental and emotional hole that they're in. A sense of powerlessness is considered to be a major contributing factor in the heightened negative stress reaction that results in an elevated cortisol response. Coping resources can compensate for the potential crippling effects of stressful events, and the construct of psychological "hardiness" is thought to buffer the negative effects of stress in these situations.

Coping is a dynamic process that essentially involves us interacting with and adjusting to our environmental circumstances, and a strong sense of control signals a positive, adaptive coping strategy that usually presents itself in one of two ways:

1. **Problem-focused coping strategies:** With this type of strategy, individuals do something active and constructive in the face of the challenge they must deal with. They take control of their own actions and thought processes as they choose to try to resolve their problem. Their focus turns to the steps they can take to make things better (the process), rather than constantly just worrying about—and complaining about—the fact that things aren't good. They tend to try to actively "fix" the situation.

2. **Emotion-focused coping strategies:** This strategy, while more passive, is directed toward gaining emotional control and understanding about the stressful event. The individual tends to "vent" about the situation, trying to understand it and come to terms with it. As they become successful in coming to terms with the issue, their perspective changes and they grow to more effectively cope with the problem. Where on the line did you put your mark?

SENSE OF COMMITMENT

To what degree do you feel you're an important part of your work and life interactions, enjoying the activities you're involved with and fully engaged in them? How committed are you to the path you're walking in your life at this moment?

The second leg of our coping skills "stool" revolves around the issue of commitment. Simply put, the more committed we are to the path we've chosen in life, the more stress-resistant we automatically become. The less we're committed to the goals and the path we've set for ourselves, the more easily we're derailed from the actions that will lead us to those goals. As a consequence, the more stress-susceptible we become.

This is how I often describe this component of our stress-coping toolkit: We're heading down life's path and we encounter a pothole—a challenging situation or life event. The pothole in question could be a serious disease, a financial setback, a difficult performance issue, etc. If we're committed to the target we're heading toward at the end of the path, if the goal burns brightly in our mind, we view the pothole or problem simply as an obstacle we must navigate on the way to our goal. This commitment fuels our perseverance, and more often than not, by diligently working at finding a solution, we overcome the obstacle in question over time and we continue our progress down the road. In your experience, how often does it happen that, as you glance in the rear-view mirror of your life and reflect on the obstacles you've been successful in overcoming, you come to realize that it was often not as bad as you thought it was going to be at the time? The committed individual is simply more stress-resistant in the face of life's many challenges.

On the other hand, the individual who is not fully committed has a vastly different *perspective* on the pothole that life puts in their way. Because the goal at the end of the road doesn't burn brightly for them, they're less likely to persevere in the face of that obstacle. They're more likely to give up because they believe the pothole represents an insurmountable obstacle and that there's no way they can get beyond it successfully. They have little confidence in their own ability to move beyond this obstacle, and the pothole becomes a barrier that prevents further progress, instead of simply being an obstacle to be navigated. Their unconscious mind then accepts that belief as reality and their emotions and behaviors adjust accordingly.

Commitment is an important tool in our coping-skills toolkit, and it comes totally from within. It cannot be imposed upon us by someone else. We, and only we, make the decision to be fully committed or not. Commitment, like integrity, can't be taken from you—you are the only one who can choose to give it up. The choice you make, however, does have an effect on how stress-resistant or stress-susceptible you become and, ultimately, on your health and performance as well. Where on the line did you put your mark?

HOW WE VIEW CHANGE

To what degree do you generally view changes in your life (whether you judge these changes to be positive or negative at the time) as a positive challenge or opportunity? To what extent do you see new situations as opportunities to grow and measure yourself against that challenge?

The relationship brought to light through the work of Holmes and Rahe informs us that humans don't "do" change very well as a general rule! That's why the magnitude of life change events has been shown to be closely related to health status. Research tells us that the individual who accepts that change is an integral part of life and indeed one of its greatest constants, and who purposefully looks for the opportunity that change most often brings, is automatically more stress-resistant than the individual who constantly and tenaciously pushes back against change.

This doesn't mean that we must necessarily like the change that's happening, but rather, when it's forced upon us by circumstances outside of our control ("B" factors), that we accept it as part of life and try to make the most out of a changing situation. The individual who rails against change, who constantly brings it up as a devastating element of their life and who resists it with every fiber of their being, is automatically more stress-susceptible when change is thrust upon them. They become angry, depressed, disillusioned, and incorrectly focused, and their negative emotional state prevents them from moving on and tackling the problem with a more optimistic, positive, and task-focused mindset. Their negative perspective drives the negative emotional stress they feel, and the systems within their body react to the negative effects of anxiety. The cortisol response is triggered, and their health and performance are more likely to deteriorate. Where on the line did you put your mark?

SENSE OF CONNECTIONS

What degree of emotional and mental support do you feel you have with respect to problems or difficulties you may confront in your life (both in work and in your personal life)? This statement reflects the human/

emotional connections you feel you can count on for support when the situation you're facing becomes difficult or challenging.

The last leg of our coping-skills stool revolves around the sense of emotional support or connection we feel with people around us. The more you feel "connected," the more to the right you put your mark on the line, the more stress-resistant you automatically tend to be. The less you feel you have emotional support when faced with a major life challenge, the more stress-susceptible you tend to be. The interesting thing about this component is that we don't have to enjoy support from a great many people, but rather that we feel a deep-rooted emotional support from someone in our life: a parent, a sibling, a spouse, a child, a coworker, a teammate, a classmate, a friend, etc. It reflects the degree to which we feel that we have someone who will backstop us if we end up in a difficult situation where we need emotional support. If we have a single individual or a pool of such people with whom we enjoy this kind of support, we tend to be more stress-resistant than if we feel that we're alone, that if something happens to us and we end up in difficulty, we're on our own.

Here's the way I often describe it: We're walking along the tightrope of life, taking steps cautiously because some of the challenges we face are significant. If we look down and see a strong, robust safety net below that's in place to catch us should we fall, we're able to more effectively remain calm and focus on taking each step to the best of our ability. We trust that if circumstances cause us to fall, we'll have the necessary emotional support we need to get back up on the wire and reengage the challenge in front of us. If, on the other hand, we look down from that high wire and only see the concrete floor, because we don't believe that we have an emotional safety net to rely on, our fear of falling and its consequences increases and we become less able to take the steps that will lead us along our path. In this situation, we might even picture ourselves falling, and our fears become crippling as we freeze in place. We become incapable of taking the steps necessary to move on.

The sad irony that underpins the very nature of our coping skills is that reality doesn't really matter in the situations I've outlined above. For each of the four variables we've discussed, it's not the reality of the situation that either causes us stress or reduces our negative stress response, but rather that it's our *perception* of that situation that most directly influences our stress response (the heart of Rule #6). It's not the activating events in our life that cause us negative stress and corrupt our health and performance, but rather, it's more about how we choose to see these things—what we choose to believe and how we cope with them—that has the greatest effect on our health and performance. If we maintain a negative mindset, we become distracted and focus on the things that are worrying us and our level of stress increases. The more effectively we can cope with stress, the more we can remain correctly focused and perform to our highest level of ability.

As you reflect on the four elements of our coping-skills toolbox, consider the moments of positive effect you could have to help your children develop their coping skills.

As life unfolds, help them to understand (in the moment) that while they may not be able to control many of the things that happen in their life, they always have full control over *how they choose to see the situation* . . . what they choose to believe about it. Over time, with this kind of consistent input from you, your child will come to realize that their perception is a choice and that this choice has tremendous power to help them get the most out of the situation or on the downside, to sabotage them by corrupting their mindset in the face of that situation. Help them to shape their perspective regarding the things that happen in their life.

Help them to realize that commitment to a goal and its attendant course of action actually makes them more stress-resistant in the face of adversity. They will come to recognize that while they can't control outcome, they are always in full control of the actions and the effort they apply to work toward the goals they've set for themselves. This mindset will make it easier for them to focus on what they're doing rather than on the outcome of their actions. The stress they feel will be less, and their personal performance will be better.

When change does occur (as it inevitably will), help them to keep change in the right perspective. It doesn't mean they have to like the fact that things are changing, but the sooner they accept it (especially when they have no choice) and look for the new opportunities it might present, the less will be the negative stress response they feel as a result of that change. Their mental and physical health will be better, as will their performance. Over time and with consistent coaching, this mindset does develop.

And finally, show them through your words and actions that, regardless of what might happen in life and the choices they might make as they move through it, you'll always be there for them. Help them to understand that life is a team sport and that you are and will always be an integral part of their team. Their unwavering belief that there's always someone in their corner who is there to help unconditionally support their emotional needs will help immunize them against the negative effects of challenging life moments and the negative stress that these might create. Stress is not a direct function of the challenges life throws in our path as much as it is a product of how we choose to see those challenges. You can help your children to see them differently.

I would now like to shift the discussion a little to discuss what the world of psychology refers to as "trait anxiety." Trait anxiety describes the predisposition that each of us has to be more or less anxious, as a general tendency. Some people, given their current situation and the perspective they choose to adopt about it, tend to be more trait anxious (often referred to as high-responders), while others tend to be less so (considered low-responders). The more trait-anxious person feels things deeply and quickly. They are emotionally reactive, and they "rev up" with little provocation. This doesn't mean they always show it to others because sometimes they work very hard to hide their feelings, but it does mean that they feel it deeply and easily. When things are good, we have to peel the high-responder off the ceiling, but when things are bad, we have to dig them out of the subbasement! Their range of emotional volatility is broad, and they tend to swing from highs to lows more easily than do low trait-anxious individuals.

The less trait-anxious person reacts to things very differently. It almost seems we have to beat on these people with a stick to get a rise out of them. We see two very different responses to the same kind of situation. These individuals are certainly capable of highs and lows, but their responses are more muted. When things are good, they tend to think, *That's great, but let's not go crazy,* but when things are bad, they tend to think, *That sucks, but let's not get carried away.* Their emotional volatility swings in a less dramatic fashion.

What does the performance literature suggest about these two individuals? In essence, the research information from the performance world informs us that the low-responder mindset is more conducive to high performance while the high-responder mindset is less likely to be associated with championship-caliber performance. Ultimately, I believe that it comes back to the Holy Grail of the Performance Equation, to the issue of *correct focus.*

The high-responder has such a broad emotional volatility that it's very difficult for these individuals to bring their focus to bear on specific things and control it to be directed to the right thing at the right time for any length of time. Their inability to sustain their focus of attention on performance-relevant thoughts and actions means that all too often they end up focusing on the wrong thing and their performance deteriorates accordingly. The low-responder, on the other hand, has a narrower range of emotional volatility, and it's much easier for that individual to control and indeed sustain their focus of attention to be on the right thing at the right time. They're not as easily pulled off task by the external and internal distracters in their environment, and their correct focus usually translates to better performance and better results.

Can we change our trait anxiety predisposition? I can tell you without reservation that we can, because I've observed such a shift in thinking in many of my clients over the years. It's simple enough in principle, although it's not always easy in practice. In a nutshell, we can accomplish this shift in our trait anxiety predisposition by doing a better job of policing our thoughts and *controlling our perspective* on the many challenging situations we encounter in life. If we become better at *eavesdropping* on our own internal mind chatter and adjusting, in some cases even challenging, our thought processes to focus more effectively on that which we can truly control (our own "A" Game), we stop worrying about the "B" factors in life and about results.

A FINAL THOUGHT CONCERNING PERSPECTIVE . . .

I'll admit that sometimes it's difficult to find the silver lining when the cloud appears so dark and overpowering. How can you change your perspective on the challenging situation in front of you when you can't think of a single positive thing about it? In this situation, you can always use my personal default thought process that goes something like this:

Well, that really sucks and I can't think of a single positive thing about this situation. But it does yet again provide me with an opportunity to see what I'm made of, to see if I have the backbone of a champion who can still bring the best he has to the situation, no matter how difficult that situation might be. It's another opportunity to measure myself against a significant challenge and see what kind of stuff I'm made of.

Simply choosing to look at the problem in this way now directs your thoughts and actions to focus on the task in front of you, and stop the mental digging that corrupts this task-focused mindset. The A.C.T. Model will explain how you can begin to move down this path.

CHAPTER 8

Rule #7

If you do what you have always done, you'll get what you have always gotten . . . If you want something different, you must approach the challenges you face with a different mindset!

If you successfully integrate the Rules of the Mental Road into your day-to-day thinking, you'll hold the secret to understanding how to program your mind for success. You'll be better able to shape and control your dominant thought so that you can more easily slip into your mental zone of ideal performance on command and, through your actions and words, transfer this understanding to your children.

Since the mind can only process one thought at a time and because you can't NOT think about whatever is on your mind, your performance will be best served by implanting a dominant-thought program in your mind that describes what you want and exactly how you perform when you excel in the act of its execution. If you focus on this mental program with intensity and single-mindedness, you'll optimize your performance and will never suffer from performance anxiety. There will be no processor capacity available to process anything other than this positive and task-focused mindset! You should now understand more clearly how you sabotage yourself and how the way that you think directly influences how you perform.

SO HOW DO YOU CHANGE?

PART TWO

The A.C.T. Model Process

Reprogramming Your Mind to Optimize Your Personal Performance

If you want to be a Champion, A.C.T. the way a Champion would act!

You may not recognize it as such, but each of us is the product of a lifetime of mental "conditioning." Whether it's in our personal lives, our professional activities, or our recreational or academic pursuits, we've been conditioned through our day-to-day experiences to exhibit behaviors that are consistent with the expectations we place on ourselves. These behaviors are invariably influenced and reinforced by feedback from our environment and from important individuals in our life. While this conditioning is often positive and productive, at times it can also be negative and counterproductive.

When it comes time to "recondition" our mental programs, however, remember that the mind is different from a computer in that we can't simply erase an old habit or mental program like we can a file on a flash drive. We must *overwrite* the old program with a new, stronger one! Negative thinking patterns can be changed only by relearning different, more effective, and productive thought patterns. To do so, we must become aware of what we want to change and then consciously repeat the new thought pattern we desire over and over again in our imagination to imprint the new belief into our unconscious mind. We need to create a new Performance Thinking habit.

In this section of the book, I'll take you through a process that will help you to develop your own A.C.T. Model, and I'll offer some thoughts about how you can adapt this approach to help your children acquire the basic elements of this philosophy of thinking, without necessarily having them create a formal model to guide their thinking.

It stands to reason that if we sometimes program ourselves in a negative way, we can also turn this thinking around to begin to reprogram ourselves positively, to exhibit behaviors that are consistent with success at the highest levels. But how do we go about reconditioning ourselves mentally to more consistently achieve this state of ideal performance often referred to as being "in the Zone"?

The goal of the A.C.T. Model process is to create and implement a mental program that serves as an automatic pilot for your behavior. By creating a model of personal excellence that allows you to preset (and then reset) your dominant thought in the moments of your performance, you'll come to think and behave in a manner that's consistent with your best performance. The A.C.T. Model process is a systematic approach that involves both self-analysis and self-correction. It's a process that incorporates and integrates basic concepts drawn from five areas of science that speak powerfully to how our mind works: Psycho-Cybernetics, Rational Emotive Behavior Therapy, Control Theory, Neuro-Linguistic Programming (NLP), and Autogenic Training. It's not my intent here to discuss each of these approaches individually, but rather to reinforce the fact that the A.C.T. Model process was not simply pulled out of thin air—there's a great deal of science that backstops the systematic approach utilized in this process.

When we designed the A.C.T. Model process several decades ago, we wanted to create a methodology that was simple, easy to implement ("doable"), and effective. My experience working with thousands of high-performance athletes, occupational professionals, and business leaders over the years affirms that the A.C.T. Model process scores well on all three counts—so much so that I offer my clients a money-back guarantee. If they hold up their end of the deal—that is, if they work with their model deliberately and purposefully for one month—and there isn't a *meaningful change* in their performance, I'll give them back every dime the program costs! Let's turn our attention now to the solution to answer the burning question:

"So How Do I Change?"

THE A.C.T. MODEL PROCESS

The A.C.T. Model acronym defines the three key steps that are used in this process of mental reconditioning. We'll address each of these steps in turn in greater detail later in this last chapter. Here's what the process looks like, as an overview:

- **"A"** Game Standards
- Compare
- Transform

"A" GAME STANDARDS: The "A" of the model identifies your personal standards of excellence, the standards that define *you* when you deliver "A" Game performances. The first step in the process demands that you understand and identify the characteristics that underlie the mindset you possess when you deliver your best performance—in a sense, your "gold" standards. Once identified, the goal of the process is ultimately to model them!

COMPARE: The "C" of the model describes the process of self-analysis that leads you to compare your actual performance in a given situation with respect to each of your standards against your target or ideal standards. This establishes a gap between your current behavior or mindset and the mindset that qualifies as your "A" Game standard. By the simple act of establishing in your mind the gap between where you were and where you wanted to be in a given situation, your unconscious mind automatically begins to reshape your emotions and behaviors to move you toward those standards of personal excellence. It's a straightforward gap-analysis technique that sets up an automatic process of correction. Your unconscious mind takes its direction from your conscious dominant thought, and the pendulum moves you in that direction.

TRANSFORM: The "T" of the model guides you in the use of "self-talk" to input a clear, defined set of dominant thoughts and images that will influence your behavior and your performance in a positive way. With controlled positive and task-relevant imagery, your own internal mental coach (that little voice in your head) will help to transform you into the performer you want to be as you shift toward this mindset associated with your best performance. Again, remember the influence of dominant thought on the movement of the pendulum.

My goal in the remaining pages of this book is to walk you through a series of steps that should allow you to create a beginner-level personal A.C.T. Model. This model will have the power to begin to change your dominant thoughts and your behavior, and with this better mental program in place, there's a greater likelihood that the wrong mental programs won't be processed (Rule #2). As you work through the creation of your own A.C.T. Model and refine the skill as you apply it to your life in general, you'll develop a deeper understanding of the process. With this greater understanding, you'll be better able to help your children to find the mindset that is associated with their best performance and learn to model it, whether it exists as an informal process when they're young or a more defined process as they get older. Let's begin to develop your personal A.C.T. Model.

CHAPTER 9

Step 1

Identify Your "A" Game Standards

The first step in the A.C.T. Model process demands that you identify the characteristics that define you when you do your BEST work (these are *your* "A" Game standards). It's impossible for me to know what business, occupation, or sport you're engaged in, so out of necessity, I'll take a more generic approach to the process in the coming pages. You'll need to apply the process to your own situation.

Find a pencil, get comfortable, and get ready to tap into some memories associated with your performance, because you're going to revisit some of your "best-ever" past performances. As you go through this exercise, imagine that there's a magic camera trained on you, watching you closely and following your every move as you engaged the action of that performance. This camera is magic because not only does it allow you to see what you looked like from the outside as you performed in these moments of personal brilliance, but it's also capable of looking inside you to understand what you were seeing in your mind's eye and what you were feeling as you executed and engaged the task. Use this analogy of a magic camera as you study yourself to understand what characteristics *define you* when you do your best work. How do you think, feel, walk, talk, move, etc. when you're on your "A" Game? What would I see if I were watching you closely? What would the magic camera tell us about you by looking inside to your thoughts and feelings when you're at your best?

Now, I want you to direct this thought process to a specific event. Think back in your past experiences to consider moments of "best-ever" performance, instances in your life where your personal performance was as good as you can ever remember it being . . . when you were truly on your "A" Game. Be clear in what I'm asking here. I don't mean times where the *result* you achieved at the end of that performance was the best-ever, but rather that your personal performance while engaged in the task was superlative, absolutely the best you were capable of delivering.

Over the years, every one of my clients have reported that some of their best performances weren't always associated with the best results they achieved, although there's usually a good correlation between moments of personal brilliance and positive outcome. Yet, there were also times when performances that netted a lower finishing position still represented a better quality of personal performance than other instances where these individuals actually finished at the top of the podium or "won." They just didn't realize the outcome they were hoping for because a "B" factor got in the way. In this exercise, we're looking for the best personal performances you've ever achieved. Pick one that stands out in your mind when you were truly "in the Zone" and recall your memories of that event. Reflect on this past experience and consider the following questions as prompts to your memory:

- When and where did the performance you're thinking of occur?
- What time of the year was it?
- What was the weather like, if that's relevant?
- What time of day did the performance occur?
- Were there any unusual or unique circumstances concerning the

event; anything important or out of the ordinary that stands out in your memory, leading up to the event in question; something that might have happened just before that competition or event to influence your mindset at that time, etc.?

- Remember as best as you can how the event unfolded, as you prepared for it, and then as you stepped into the event ready to engage the task in front of you.

As you consider this best-ever experience, use the form presented in Table 1 and write in descriptive words or adjectives that reflect the set of mental images, thoughts, and feelings that exactly define *what you're like, how you think,* and *who you are* when you're mentally "in the Zone." I don't want to put words in your mouth, but here are some examples of descriptors that could be used: aggressive, serene, deliberate, centered, smooth, focused, calm, etc. Take the time to work through this individual brainstorming process carefully since it's the foundation that you'll build upon to create your model. You're in effect creating a mind-map associated with moments of personal virtuosity. This exercise may take you 15–20 minutes to complete. Please don't read any further until you've completed this process.

Assuming you've completed the exercise as I laid it out in the previous paragraph, take a moment to reflect on how you feel right now. As you thought back to this best-ever experience and sought to understand (and put words to describe) the mindset, emotions, and feelings associated with that experience, did you begin to feel differently? If you engaged in the exercise fully, it's likely that working through it caused you to feel more like that individual who, on the day of that performance, delivered a great performance. It's likely that your mindset shifted to become more aligned with the mindset that existed when you performed to the best of your ability. Again, the pendulum moved. This is the power of dominant thought and the essence of the A.C.T. Model process.

TABLE 1: DESCRIPTORS THAT DEFINE ME WHEN I DO MY BEST WORK!

I asked you to complete this task before reading on because the descriptors or words that connect to the mindset associated with virtuosity *for you* must come *from you*. They must be your words. Because we can't accomplish this task as an interactive process, I'd like to share with you what, based on my experience, many individuals often identify as characteristics that define them when they're at their best. This may help you to refine your personal model.

It has been clear from my experience over the years that there are common threads or themes that the majority of people involved in the high-performance world share with respect to the state of mind they possess when they do their best work. This observation is also supported in the research literature regarding flow state and performance. My experience confirms that it doesn't matter what language they speak, what culture they're from, what their gender is, what their sport or job might be, *or* how old they are; the mindset associated with excellence seems to be built from a surprisingly common platform.

To put structure to that platform, a number of years ago I examined the A.C.T. Models of more than a thousand high-performance clients to extract and aggregate the descriptors that most commonly seemed to be reported by them as being associated with their moments of best-ever performance.

While not everyone identifies all of these basic behaviors as part of their personal model of excellence and many individuals identify other variables that are not part of this common framework, there's enough consistency in these profiles for me to pull together eight common themes that seem to be associated with the mindset that exists when people are "in the Zone." These themes aren't universal, but the frequency of their representation in the high-performance population would be astounding to most people I expect, until you begin to consider the Rules of the Mental Road and how they impact performance. I suspect that many of the words or at least the "intent" of those words that you listed in Table 1 might ultimately be found in this common list. Let's now consider these common themes:

The Basic Behaviors That Underlie Excellence in Performance

- **calm;** relaxed; loose; cool; rested; at peace; detached; unflappable; in harmony; comfortable; composed; free; heavy; breathe; fulfilled; serene; tranquil; chill; secure; grateful; quiet; blissful; emotionless; neutral
- **focused;** here and now; single-minded; in my shell; clear-headed; centered; sharp; tuned-in; alert; in the moment; non-judgmental; fully present; locked in; connected; zeroed in; clairvoyant; issue at hand; alone; head up

- **confident;** arrogant; bullet-proof; powerful; strong; walking tall; cocky; dominant; positive; self-assured; believe; connected; courageous; bold; well-prepared; capable; invincible; committed; superior; the man; empowered; puffed out; trust; certain; no doubt
- **energized;** pumped-up; revved-up; passionate; joyful; challenged; enthusiastic; fun; excited; motivated; alive
- **aggressive;** tenacious; persistent; intense; unstoppable; hungry; on the edge; assertive; predator; purposeful; relentless; decisive; panther; lion; shark; dedicated; determined; fearless; pushing the limit; Alpha
- **smooth;** rhythm; fluid; flow; effortless; easy; nimble; tempo; slow motion; efficient
- **anticipate;** analytical; opportunistic; adaptable; smart; adaptive; flawless; sensitive; calculating; open-minded; flexible; aware; cunning
- **in control;** in command; measured; selfish; patient; professional; responsible; inspiring; precise; methodical; deliberate; persuasive; manipulating; Machiavellian; chameleon; leader; balanced; poised; take charge; convincing; accurate

I've organized these sets of descriptors around a particular word I've bolded and placed at the beginning of each grouping. Note, however, that there's no predominance of these words over any of the other words in the group. They are simply meant to encapsulate the underlying behavior or theme that is highlighted by the different words used in that category. For example, some people prefer the word "calm" as a descriptor in their model, whereas others might prefer the words "serene" or "at peace" to convey the sense that there is an absence of "noise" in their head when they do their best work. The correct descriptor for each person is the word that connects that person most powerfully to the images, feelings, and memories of what the state of mind represents for them when they're at the top of their game. Compare your words with this list. Are any of your words shared by others?

One of the striking things that stands out when we examine the list of descriptors above is that every one of these words speaks to an element of mindset or behavior associated with execution, an in-the-moment oriented thought process. This is in sharp contrast to words that would reference an outcome or a result such as coming in first, being the fastest, winning the race, getting the gold medal, etc.

It's indeed revealing that virtually all of these very successful high-performance competitors associate words that describe thoughts and emotions that relate directly to the quality of their execution (the "A" in our "A" × "B" = Results Performance Equation) rather than thoughts that represent a concern for or a focus on "B" factors, or even on "Results," when they perform to the best of their ability. This observation simply reinforces the fact that when we perform at our best, our focus of attention is necessarily directed toward the act of execution itself and not to the outcome we hope to see materialize. When they're in their "Zone" of best performance, it appears that high-level competitors are indeed connected to what they're doing and fully engaged by the process of that execution. I would now like to take a few moments to briefly address the eight basic behaviors that seem to underlie the performance mindset of many high-level competitors:

Calm: This is a recurring theme that's highlighted in virtually every A.C.T. Model I've reviewed in one form or another. If you think about it, this makes sense. It's very difficult for us to "hear" our inner voice talking to us and be guided by it to process the correct thoughts when our head is filled with "noise." When there's emotional upheaval, anxiety, and excessive mind chatter, it's really difficult to control and sustain our focus of attention on anything for any length of time. A sense of mental or emotional calm is a necessary prerequisite/corequisite to the other underlying behaviors that appear to be part of the common framework for a high-performance mindset.

Focused: If you think back to your best-ever performances, you'll probably recognize that your focus was directed fully on the task in front of you and controlled by you, to attend only to execution-relevant information and decisions. It's not surprising to see that one of the descriptors used in virtually every A.C.T. Model addresses what I described previously as the Holy Grail of the Performance Equation—the ability to focus in the moment on the task at hand to the exclusion of all else. As you'll recall, this was one of the two things (the other being about confidence) that my clients routinely seek when they visit with me. It would be very difficult to explain why the word "focus," and by focus, I mean *correct focus* or *task focus,* would NOT be part of an individual's personal performance model.

Confident: The confidence that high-performance people talk about as being associated with their best work usually revolves around confidence in the knowledge and belief that they "can" be successful, not necessarily confident that they "will" be. While many report they "knew" they would win, even in those situations their confidence seems to be more about the belief that they can handle whatever the situation throws at them and that they can overcome it. It's a supreme confidence in self. If we lack self-confidence and begin to doubt ourselves, our focus of attention naturally shifts to what it is that we're worried about, and we end up focusing on the wrong thing. The end result is that our personal performance is less effective than it could have been, regardless of the outcome we might achieve.

Energized: A sense of energy, enthusiasm, or excitement is often associated with the "A" Game performances of high-level competitors. This is where the aspect of "fun" lives, and the passion they feel for the occupation, activity, or sport they're undertaking serves as emotional fuel that allows them to put in the ongoing effort required to be at the top of their game. It takes a great deal of energy to sustain our focus of attention for an extended period of time (as we can all attest to, it's difficult to sustain a strong mental focus when we're physically fatigued), and the sense of energy that's associated with a championship mindset supports our ability to focus effectively. Have you ever delivered an "A" Game performance when you felt sluggish or washed out? I suspect not.

Aggressive: The aggressiveness that's associated with the typical A.C.T. Model is not usually directed toward someone else. It's not about the competitor being angry or aggressive in the common sense of the word. Rather, it reflects an elevated level of intensity where the performer is "pushing the envelope" somewhat. Often, clients talk about the need for patience so that they don't overreach but follow that up with a recognition that they can't be *too* patient or they'll get left behind. The trick is to be *just patient enough* to operate within their level of control but push hard enough to be in a position to capitalize on an opponent's mistake or even make things happen as well. It does set up a seemingly interesting contradiction, however.

The first descriptor we examined from the typical A.C.T. Model was "calm," and yet in the paragraph above, I identify the word "aggressive" as also being a common trait when we perform "in the Zone." These two words seem to conflict with each other. How can we be both calm and aggressive at the same time? If you think about the moments when you've been in that "Zone" of best performance, you'll recognize that there's a blend of these two traits that can coexist nicely. It's indeed possible to be emotionally calm but physically and mentally intense at the same time, and when we're able to hit this "sweet spot," performing at a high level becomes somewhat effortless, even though we're potentially expending a great deal of energy.

What you must do is figure out what the blend of these two traits is that optimizes your performance, given what it is that you do when you're in that moment of performance. Some activities might require a little higher level of intensity, usually when more physically powerful, gross motor tasks are involved, or a lower level of intensity, when the task involves fine motor skills and dexterity, for example. Of course, different people require different levels of "mental activation." Use the two gauges in Figure 9 to visually represent the level of activation that seems to optimize your performance.

For reference, on the "calm" gauge, "0" means you're in a coma and "10K" represents the most wound up you've ever been in your life. You're hitting your personal rev limiter and are maxed out! Calm doesn't even exist in your vocabulary when you're at this end of the scale. On the "intensity" gauge, "0" means that you are completely flat, that you are totally passive, while "10K" on the scale represents a level of intensity that is as high as you are humanly capable of achieving. You're over the top! Where does your unconscious mind tell you that you should put your mark on each of these gauges?

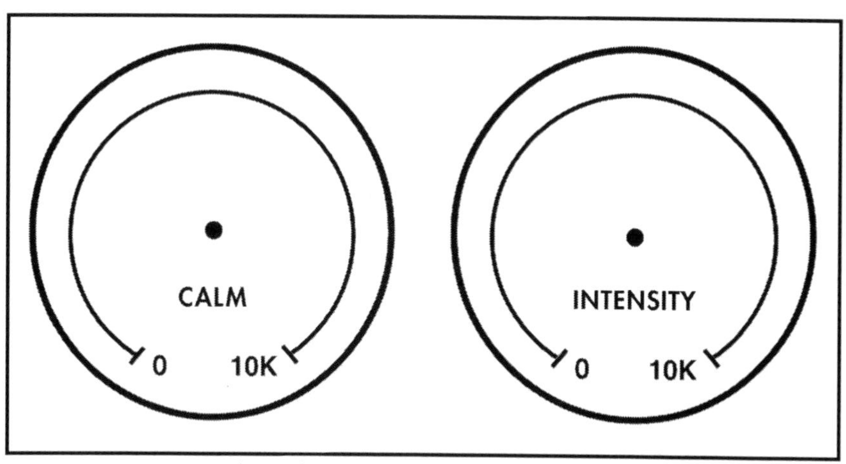

Figure 9: The Relationship Between Calm and Intensity When You Do Your BEST Work

The identification of the specific level of these two traits really is an individual thing. Some people require a different level of psychological activation than do others, and neither is correct nor incorrect. The goal is for you to identify the levels that optimize your performance so that you can work on clearly defining the state of mind associated with these two characteristics and learn how to bring yourself to that level on command, using your personal A.C.T. Model. It's important to understand the fundamental difference between being "tense," which is a bad thing generally and "intense," which is often a good thing. If you can describe it and picture it with clarity in your own mind, you can model it!

I've discussed this juxtaposition of calm and intensity with my high-performance clients on many occasions, and there is again a relatively narrow window that seems to be common to most of them when they perform at the highest level (illustrated in Figure 10). There is an optimal range that most speak about that is relatively consistently associated with the times in their competitive life when they deliver their best performances. Here is what they report:

On the "calm" side of the ledger, they speak about an optimal level at around 4,000 on the dial (where the range of responses

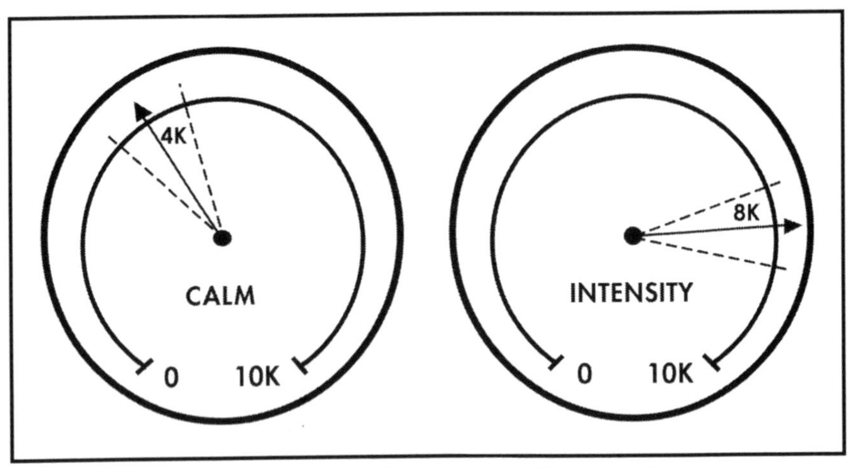

Figure 10: The Relationship Between Calm and Intensity for Many in the High-Performance World

might typically vary from 3,500 to 4,500 on our 10,000 point scale). It's clear that when they do their best work, there is indeed a sense of internal quiet that is evident (there is an absence of mental "noise'), and this picture is consistent with the assertion that most people perform at their best when they're NOT anxious and preoccupied. Of course, we now know that one of the important reasons for this basic truth is that when we're anxious, our focus of attention shifts away from what we should be focused on to what it is that we're worried about, and that incorrect focus directly affects our performance. When you're at your best, how does your level compare to theirs? If you look at yourself with the eye of our magic camera, what does it see when you're in this good place?

On the "intensity" side of the ledger, my clients often speak about an optimal level of around 8,000 on the scale, where the range of responses typically varies from 7,500 to 8,500, depending on the person and the situation they're in. These numbers are simply a representation, a "gut" feeling if you will, of the intensity level they operate at when they perform to the best of their ability.

It's again clear that their intensity, even in the *most intense situations,* is generally not at the top end of the scale. It's dialed back somewhat from the most extreme intensity they're capable of. They report that if they're *too* intense, if they're pushing too hard or overdriving the situation, their performance suffers. What they're generally looking to find is that sweet spot where they feel somewhat emotionally calm but are capable of a high level of physical and mental intensity. This isn't an easy place to find, but it can help to think about it in this way.

Unfortunately, what often happens (as illustrated in Figure 11) is that with the increasing worry we sometimes feel, especially when we focus on results and the results are not what we'd hoped they'd be, a calm mindset slips through our fingers. The needle on the "calm" gauge starts to creep to the right. Unfortunately, the natural response to this loss of calm and the increase in anxiety that it reflects is that our intensity also begins an upward creep,

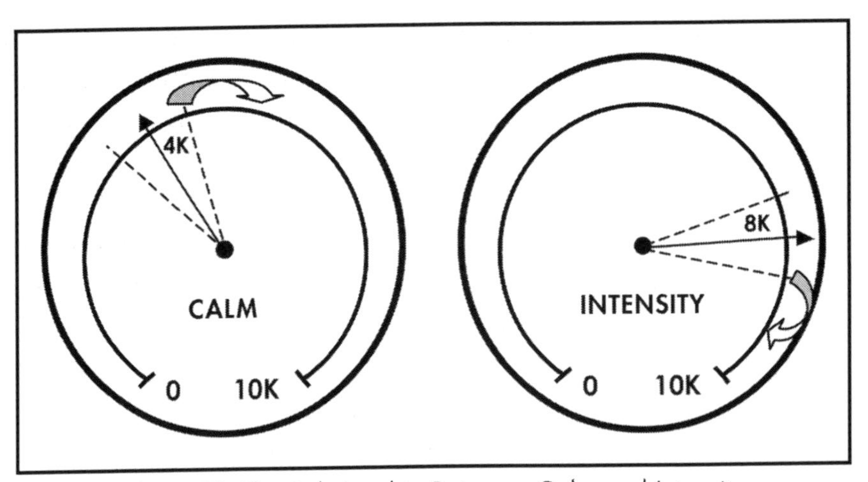

Figure 11: The Relationship Between Calm and Intensity When a Loss of Calm/Increase in Anxiety Occurs

and we end up "overreaching" or "trying too hard." Our performance is usually never as good as it is when we work within that sweet spot.

Smooth: There is a sense of flow or rhythm to superlative performances. Whether I'm speaking with a combat pilot, a racecar driver, a golfer, a surgeon, a musician, or a sales professional, they describe a feeling of rhythm or tempo that helps to connect them intimately to the execution of the performance in which they're engaged. The more they can tap into this sense of rhythm, the better their focus on the task and the more they seem to be able to execute with smooth precision. Execution feels "effortless."

Anticipate: My clients speak about a sense of keen awareness that provides them with a mental reserve of processing capacity that allows them to adapt instantly to the evolving situation in their surrounding environment. Things sometime seem to happen in slow motion. When they're "in the Zone," they seem to be able to anticipate how the situation or performance will evolve, seemingly aware of what's going to happen even before it does. It's almost like they become somewhat clairvoyant.

In Control: When they're operating at their best, my clients talk about being in complete control of themselves, fully on top of every action they undertake. They're precise and accurate in their movements, deliberate in the way they execute. Everything happens as they will it to happen. Even if they recognize they can't control other things, it almost seems as though they can. Their thought process seems to directly influence what happens around them. They're so connected to what's happening in the moment that they become the controlling agent in their environment.

Now that we've briefly overviewed the underlying behaviors that are frequently included in a personal A.C.T. Model, it's time for you to take the list of descriptors you identified in the earlier exercise (from Table 1) and whittle it down into a list of the six to nine key variables that define who you are when you do your best work. There's no magic number in the A.C.T. Model, however. Some individuals feel that their model is more effective if they have a greater number of keywords while others feel that theirs is more effective when they have fewer.

The downside of having too few descriptors in your model is that you might miss important underlying behaviors that could serve to connect you more powerfully to the state of mind associated with your best performances. The downside of having too many, on the other hand, is that the model becomes unwieldy and cumbersome. As such, the reflection you undertake when you consider these descriptors in your conscious mind becomes repetitious and blurs together because you have different words that are really speaking to the same quality or behavior. When you have too many words in your model, it's more difficult to fully implement the model, especially at the beginning. It must be simple and relatively easy to engage if the model is to be effective. It appears that, for most people, a model that includes six to nine descriptors seems to work well.

The first step to begin to compress your set of personal descriptors into a functional A.C.T. Model is to look at your list and identify the words that speak to the same quality, grouping them together along common themes. For example, if you had included the words "calm," "still," "quiet," etc. in your long list of words, these would likely fit within the same category. You can use a form with a structure similar to that of Table 2 to aggregate your words around common themes:

TABLE 2: GROUPED A.C.T. MODEL DESCRIPTORS

Calm	Still
Serene	Quiet
Tranquil	At Peace
. . .	. . .
Intense	Revved Up
Predator	Aggressive
Unstoppable	. . .
. . .	. . .
. . .	. . .

Once you've extracted the common themes from the personal descriptors you previously identified from your best-ever past performance experiences, sit back and examine the groups carefully. Are there other qualities or behaviors that you missed in your list that would be important to include? Are there other words that could be included within each category that might be more effective and powerful at connecting you to the quality you're examining? Once you're comfortable with your list of words and feel that they represent the key behaviors that are associated with the mindset *you* possess when you do your best work, the next step is to pick the one word from each category that you think is the most powerful descriptor for you. The word you select should be the one that connects you most strongly to the thoughts, memories, images, and feelings that define you when you're on your "A" Game, *relative to that behavior.* Circle that word. You now have a keyword or descriptor that identifies an important behavior or quality you can associate clearly with thoughts and feelings that exist when you're in your Zone of best performance. You may also have a list of secondary level words that speak to the same quality or behavior but that are not quite as meaningful or powerful at connecting you to that behavior.

The A.C.T. Model isn't a checklist. It's not a set of words you remind yourself of occasionally and do the mental equivalent of "checking the box." Rather, it's a process where the words of your A.C.T. Model serve as portals to direct your dominant thought to reflect on the memories, images, and feelings associated with that descriptor, when you're operating at the top of your game. We can use the simple analogy of a room (as illustrated in Figure 12) to describe the process of what we're trying to accomplish.

Imagine a room with a door on which a sign is affixed. The word painted onto the sign is the key descriptor for the behavior you're seeking to model in your personal A.C.T. Model. Let's

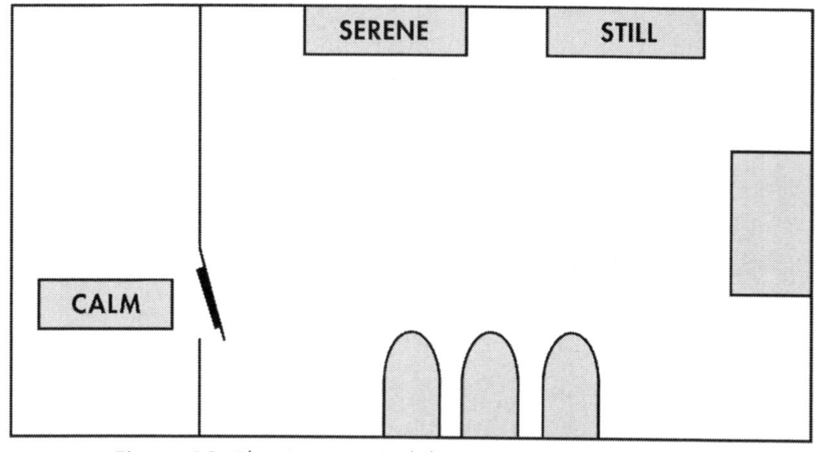

Figure 12: The A.C.T. Model Room Analogy Imagery

assume for the purpose of discussion that the word on one of the doors is "CALM." As we stand outside the room, we consider for a moment what "CALM" represents for us when we're operating at the top of our game. As we step into this room (in our mind's eye), we observe different things. There are other signs on the wall that feature the words "SERENE" and "STILL." They give depth, texture, and color to the meaning of the word "CALM." They help us to remember the nuances of what "CALM" feels like when we're on our game.

There are other things in the room as well. The square-looking shape might represent a clear memory of a past performance experience where we were at the *perfect* level of calmness, a moment of performance excellence for us. The rounded-looking shapes might represent different illustrations that clarify "CALM" in different ways: waves lapping quietly on the seashore; breathing that is labored and tense becoming slow, shallow, and relaxed; a graphic equalizer from a stereo that moves from a series of wild gyrations to a baseline level as our mind finds the perfect level of "CALM" that optimizes our performance; the needle on the "calm" gauge being positioned at exactly the right spot, etc. It's simply a process to guide your imagery and, ultimately, your dominant thought so that your unconscious mind can begin to move you in that direction and bring you to a state of emotional calm that supports your ability to perform to the best of your ability.

Now that you've completed this refinement process, list your key descriptors in Table 3. Don't worry about the order of the words; we'll tackle this task next.

The next step in developing your personal A.C.T. Model is to establish the most effective progression of thought for the descriptors listed—the order of the words in your model. You'll need to establish the order you believe is most appropriate for you. Let me offer some food for thought that should help you in defining the most appropriate order. I will, however, come at it from what might seem like a strange direction.

TABLE 3: MY PERSONAL A.C.T. MODEL

Many years ago, there was a weekly television series that featured the adventures of Superman, a character who was born from an action comic. When Superman's alter ego, Clark Kent, received "the call" that someone was in distress and needed help, there was a series of actions set into motion that led him through a transformation process that took him from the persona of Clark Kent to that of Superman. If you saw this show, do you remember what started the process?

The first thing that Clark Kent did was "rip" off his glasses with one hand from the right to the left and then immediately pulled at his collar and tie to begin to loosen the knot as he darted off camera. We saw just a peek of the blue suit he wore underneath. Then the camera picked up Superman in his full costume as he bounded out of a window or off a balcony, accompanied by the characteristic *whoosh* that came to represent his taking to flight. The transformation or metamorphosis of Clark Kent to Superman always happened the same way. There was a progression of action that was at the core of this transformation, and it started with him taking off his glasses in a certain way.

The transformation that is initiated by the A.C.T. Model process is not unlike the metamorphosis of the fantasy character of Superman, except that instead of a progression of action involved in the transformation, it's a progression of thought. It sets into motion a new, systematic, and powerful dominant thought program that's directly connected to execution and to the mindset that exists when we perform to the highest level of our ability.

We can illustrate this progression of thought by integrating the concept of the room I described previously with the idea of a suite of rooms connected by a long corridor. It would look like the illustration in Figure 13.

For the vast majority of the A.C.T. Models I have guided individuals to develop over the years, there have been a couple of principles that seem to hold true for almost everyone. The first principle is that most of my clients select a descriptor that speaks to the issue of emotional calmness or the absence of mental noise as the first element in their personal model. This occurs regardless of what the actual word might be that represents that state of mind for them and regardless of the activity in which they're engaged. We first need to still the noise in our head so that we can properly hear that little voice, and then direct our mind to process the right things. I believe that this same logic explains why most forms of the ancient martial arts, which involve high-intensity, one-on-one fighting, begin the process of combat with a period of meditation and relaxation to "quiet the spirit." This practice is also common in many other sports and high-risk/high-demand occupations.

The second principle is that the early part of the model tends to highlight behaviors that are more general in nature and speaks to the mindset that's optimal in the competitive environment generally. Elements of the model that come later tend to focus on behaviors that are quite specific to the process of execution that's employed in the moment of their actual performance. It's difficult to explain this progression in the abstract, so I'll use a sample of an actual person's A.C.T. Model to help illustrate the point (presented in Table 4 on page 134).

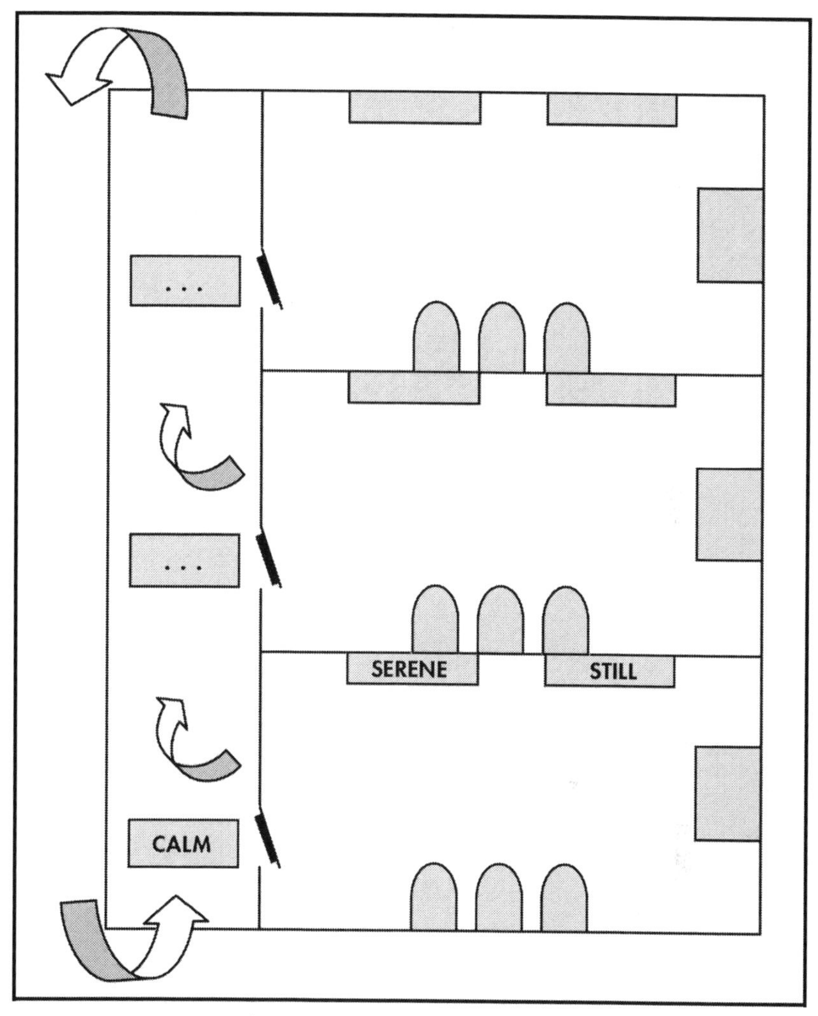

Figure 13: The A.C.T. Model Suite Analogy Imagery

TABLE 4: A SAMPLE A.C.T. MODEL
SERENE
CONFIDENT
PASSIONATE
INSPIRING
ENGAGED
MACHIAVELLIAN
FULLY PRESENT
PREDATOR

The model begins with the word "serene." It signals a quieting of mental noise and an adjustment of the "calm" dial to the optimal level for that individual, and the performance in which they're engaged. This applies not only to the moment of performance, but in the period leading up to and surrounding the actual performance. It serves as an immunization (like a vaccine) against anxiety and worry.

"Confident" reflects the sense of belief-in-self that this individual feels, recognizing that they have the knowledge, skill, and ability to get the job done. While they know they can't control the outcome of their performance, when they are in their good place, they're confident they can handle whatever the competitive environment throws at them and likely prevail.

"Passionate" reflects the sense of enthusiasm and joy they experience when they're engaged in what they're doing. This passion they have for what they do is the fuel they use to energize themselves, to continue to persevere and put in the effort necessary to be at the top of their game. It reminds them that they're doing this because, fundamentally, they love what they do. When it's not fulfilling and no longer any fun, they generally don't do their best work. The first three elements of this individual's model speak to a set of important behaviors that preface their ability to be at the top of their game. It applies not just in the moment of the performance itself, but in the window of time that surrounds that moment as well.

The word "inspiring" reflects the ability of this individual to lead, to effectively influence others to accept their point of view and come along for the ride. This descriptor begins to lean toward the actual performance, describing the individual's impact (from a distance) on others involved in the performance.

"Engaged" describes the sense of connection the individual feels with respect to others involved in the performance and to the task in which they're engaged. They do their best work when they're fully connected to the others around them and "all in" from a commitment point of view.

The term "Machiavellian" is often thought of as a negative one in that the common meaning associated with this term is that of a manipulator, something that's generally not thought of as being positive. For this individual, however, this term signals an expertise and an ability to effectively manipulate the individual(s) they're involved with, but it is very much a positive term in that it speaks to their ability to control the flow of the performance and many aspects of the performance environment itself, to create a win-win situation for everyone.

The phrase "fully present" directs this individual to the specific task-focus that is the Holy Grail of the Performance Equation. Nothing else matters but what's happening in the moment of their performance. They're not partially present when their on their "A" Game; they're fully and completely engaged in the here and now!

"Predator" rounds out this individual's model. This word aggregates all of the behaviors that are important to this individual into one metaphor: someone who is mentally and emotionally calm but is capable of high levels of intensity when called for; patient enough, but aggressive when it's required; intimately connected to the others in their environment and in control of the situation around them; and fully focused on what's happening in front of them as they wait for the exact, right moment to act!

Of course this is only one example of a model, but it serves to show a progression of thought that allows someone to move from a state of internal quiet, where their mind is unencumbered by unimportant or disruptive information to a mindset where not only do they remain calm, but they're task-focused and capable of ruthless execution when necessary. Just so you know, the individual in this example is a coach/educator.

While younger children aren't likely to understand this process from an intellectual point of view, you can still help them to begin to establish a mental model that will allow them to better control their dominant thought. You can accomplish this by "catching" them doing things correctly and bringing the mindset associated with this elevated performance state to their conscious attention.

When they generate a great performance, get them to talk about it after the fact. Ask them to describe how it felt when they were in this good place and listen carefully to the words they use to describe it. Remember, the most powerful words for them are the ones they themselves use to describe their thoughts and feelings when they're at the top of their game. As they're explaining to you what it felt like and what they were thinking in the moment of that performance, take the time to share with them what you observed when they delivered it. What you're trying to do is help them to establish a repertoire of words that become linked to images and feelings that are associated with the state of mind that exists when they are at their best.

Understand as well that certain characteristics are commonly described in these moments of virtuosity by most individuals and steer them gently in this direction if they're having trouble finding the words. Don't give them the words directly but make it easy for them to find those words on their own. For example, behaviors such as calm, confident, focused fully on what they were doing, having fun, the absence of worry, a sense of freedom, and fully engaged are characteristics that you probably observed in them and that they actually felt in those moments of virtuosity.

Help them to put words to it so that they can use these words as triggers to help them to reconnect to this state of mind in future performances. Use the descriptors they have shared to help bring them back to this place and allow the pendulum to move for them. In effect, you're helping them to create a simple imagery-based script they can then use to help get them into the state of mind that optimizes their performance. If you couple this with reminders that they can't control outcome so they should focus simply on what they *can* control—their performance—they are more likely to focus on that performance and deliver their best work. The more this state of mind becomes clear to them and the more they turn their attention to the execution of the task in front of them, the better they will do. It's simple enough, but just not very easy to do.

To facilitate this process, here are a few leading questions you can use to get the ball rolling:

- "You did a great job out there today, Susie . . . It really looked like you were in the groove! What did it feel like?"
- "When you were making your push to the goal, Tom, I was watching your face and how you were moving. . . . What were you thinking at that moment?"
- "That was a great "at bat," Wendy, in a pressure-filled situation. We really needed that home run and yet you looked relaxed! What were you thinking about as you were waiting for the pitch?"
- "When you're at your best, Billy, you get this look on your face. What goes through your mind. . . . What are you thinking when you're in that special place?"
- "You had a great game tonight, Ann! One of the best performances I've seen you have in a while. What were you thinking

about in the lead-up to the game and how would you describe yourself as the game unfolded for you?"

- "You rocked that inning, Ben! That was quite a show you put on. . . . Watching you, I got the sense you didn't have a care in the world. What did it feel like to be in that sweet spot? How would you describe yourself in that moment?"
- "That was a championship-caliber performance, Christy! You destroyed your opponents, and it looked effortless. You get this aura about you when you're 'in the Zone,' and it says a lot about what you're thinking. How would you describe yourself when you are in that good place? What do you feel like when you're there?"

At this stage of the process, you should now have established the order of your initial A.C.T. Model descriptors (transpose them into Table 5) and should be ready to begin to utilize your model of personal excellence to shape and reshape your dominant thought and your performance. Now, on to the second step in the process!

TABLE 5: MY PERSONAL A.C.T. MODEL

CHAPTER 10

Step 2

Compare Your Behaviors and Thinking Relative to Your "A" Game Standards

The second step in the A.C.T. Model process involves a systematic self-analysis of your performance, particularly in the early days of the model. In essence, once you've established your personal "A" Game standards, you utilize these standards as a model to shape (in advance of your performance) and reshape (following your performance) your dominant thoughts associated with that performance.

The shaping part comes into play before you even engage your performance. You accomplish this by imagining what you look and feel like when you're at the top of your game, as you engage the task in front of you. Put yourself in that frame of mind in your imagination. In other words, use imagery to engage your "A" Game standards and let those standards possess you! By thinking about and picturing the qualities that define excellence in you, and by using your A.C.T. Model as a framework in your conscious mind, you automatically establish the correct mindset that ultimately guides your unconscious mind to execute that program. The pendulum moves. It's really that simple, even though it requires discipline to purposefully and deliberately engage the process.

The reshaping part comes into play after the performance has been completed and it's time to evaluate how well you did. In this process of self-analysis, you compare the behaviors and mindset that defined you during the performance you just completed versus your personal model of excellence. You answer the simple question: "How did I do in that moment of performance, relative to my 'A' Game standard for that behavior or quality?"

For each descriptor in your personal model, compare where you were relative to where you wanted to be in the performance you just completed. If there was a difference, establish or define the gap in your mind by scoring that difference. Understand what the *difference* was between how you performed and how you wanted to perform for each of your standards of excellence during that event. You can create a logbook or journal to put structure to this systematic self-analysis process and use a form like that shown in Figure 14 to complete the evaluation. Put a single mark across the line based on your subjective feeling to establish the quality of your actual performance versus your ideal performance standard for that behavior (I've placed *two* marks on the line, but I'll explain why in a moment).

FIGURE 14: A.C.T. MODEL EXAMPLE OF STANDARDS OF EXCELLENCE

POOR ———————————————— IDEAL

__________ CALM __________

1 - 2 - 3 - 4 - 5 - 6| - 7 - |8 - 9

__________ . . . . __________

1 - 2 - 3 - 4 - 5 - 6 - 7 - 8 - 9

My Personal Performance

1 - 2 - 3 - 4 - 5 - 6 - 7 - 8 - 9

You'll note that in Figure 14, the line for each A.C.T. Model descriptor is anchored by the numbers "1" (POOR) and "9" (IDEAL). A "1" on the scale means that the quality of your performance was the *worst it's ever been,* while a "9" on the scale means the *best it's ever been:* ideal, perfect, exactly where you wanted to be! Realize that a "9" doesn't mean the most that you've ever been. In our example, we can use the first descriptor—"CALM"—to clarify this point further. In some performance situations, you don't want to be as calm as you've ever been because being too calm may cause you to be lethargic (remember, the ideal level on our "calm" dial was around 4,000, not 0 or even 1,000 for most individuals) and that would not optimize your performance. A "9" on this scale would indicate that the performance unfolded at *exactly the right level* of calmness for the situation. If you're either too high or too low on the "calm" dial, it's not ideal and therefore wouldn't be scored as a "9." There should be a gap where the size of the gap gives an indication of how far off your ideal you were.

In the abbreviated form in Figure 14, I placed two marks across the line to give you a sense of reference. One of the marks is just short of the "8" on the scale while the other is just to the right of the "6" on the scale. It should be clear that both marks establish a gap between their respective positions and the "9" on our scale, but it's obvious that placing the mark near the "8" means you were much closer to the ideal level of calmness for the situation than you would have been if you'd placed your mark near the "6." There isn't much of a shift required in your internal level of calmness to move yourself into that sweet spot referenced earlier when you're close to "8" versus when you're near the "6." The difference between where you were and where you wanted to be is smaller and closer to the ideal.

You'll also note that at the bottom of Figure 14, there's a statement that reads: "My Personal Performance." Use the same type of gap analysis to evaluate and highlight the strength of your *overall performance.* This isn't a reflection of how successful you were in achieving your goal (in the meeting or the presentation, for example), or how well you placed in the competition, or how high your finishing position was, but rather, it's intended to reflect the overall *quality* of the performance you delivered, in comparison to that which you would have delivered had you truly been on your "A" Game. I've included an example of what the full form might look like in Figure 15, for your reference.

FIGURE 15: PERSONAL A.C.T. MODEL—STANDARDS OF *EXCELLENCE*

POOR ——————————————— IDEAL

____

1 - 2 - 3 - 4 - 5 - 6 - 7 - 8 - 9

____

1 - 2 - 3 - 4 - 5 - 6 - 7 - 8 - 9

____

1 - 2 - 3 - 4 - 5 - 6 - 7 - 8 - 9

____

1 - 2 - 3 - 4 - 5 - 6 - 7 - 8 - 9

____

1 - 2 - 3 - 4 - 5 - 6 - 7 - 8 - 9

____

1 - 2 - 3 - 4 - 5 - 6 - 7 - 8 - 9

____

1 - 2 - 3 - 4 - 5 - 6 - 7 - 8 - 9

____

1 - 2 - 3 - 4 - 5 - 6 - 7 - 8 - 9

My Personal Performance

1 - 2 - 3 - 4 - 5 - 6 - 7 - 8 - 9

Figure 16, sharing a similar layout, is designed to pull together some *general* behaviors that are common to individuals who perform at a high level and which are important for all of us to master. Some of the elements listed in this form may not always apply since the situation you're evaluating might not lend itself to including them. If this is the case, simply leave them blank and pick only those elements that are relevant to the performance you're actually evaluating, or change them to suit your needs.

Keep in mind that what we're discussing here is a process, and as such, it can apply to any action or performance you undertake in any aspect of your life. By adopting this type of self-analysis process—either formally with a logbook using forms like those described here or informally, just undertaking the analysis in your own mind—this approach can help you to perform that task at a higher level. You just have to determine what the standards of excellence are *for you* performing that task and then use the A.C.T. Model process to help you clarify and implement what you need to change within yourself to execute that task more effectively.

Since your unconscious mind takes its direction from your conscious thought, you're effectively reprogramming your mind by using performance-based imagery that reflects the thoughts and feelings associated with how you think and feel when you do your BEST work. The "compare" step of the A.C.T. Model process requires that you execute a simple gap analysis in answer to the question: "How did I do in this performance situation?" Placing a mark across the line for each of the descriptors in your personal model of excellence establishes that gap in performance for each element and sets up the next and final step of the process.

This gap-analysis process is one that you can help your child to perform informally as well. On the heels of every performance, ask your child how they think they did with respect to their own performance (not with respect to the results they achieved, because those are obvious). You're trying to get them to honestly critique the quality of their performance and put it into perspective with respect to the results that the performance yielded. If the results were affected by a "B" factor that was out of their control, do they recognize it as such? If not, you can help them to reshape their perspective and help them to realize that their performance may actually have been very good, but the results never materialized because something outside of their control influenced the outcome. If their performance was lackluster because they were not in the game and mentally engaged, it gives them an opportunity to put the deficit in their performance into perspective using the key elements of their own informal performance model.

FIGURE 16: GENERAL BEHAVIORS

POOR ——————————————— **IDEAL**

GENERAL MOOD CONTROL
1 - 2 - 3 - 4 - 5 - 6 - 7 - 8 - 9

PHYSICAL STRESS CONTROL
1 - 2 - 3 - 4 - 5 - 6 - 7 - 8 - 9

MENTAL STRESS CONTROL
1 - 2 - 3 - 4 - 5 - 6 - 7 - 8 - 9

ANGER CONTROL
1 - 2 - 3 - 4 - 5 - 6 - 7 - 8 - 9

NUTRITIONAL DISCIPLINE
1 - 2 - 3 - 4 - 5 - 6 - 7 - 8 - 9

COMMUNICATION
1 - 2 - 3 - 4 - 5 - 6 - 7 - 8 - 9

ORGANIZATION
1 - 2 - 3 - 4 - 5 - 6 - 7 - 8 - 9

PROBLEM SOLVING ABILITY
1 - 2 - 3 - 4 - 5 - 6 - 7 - 8 - 9

____
1 - 2 - 3 - 4 - 5 - 6 - 7 - 8 - 9

CHAPTER 11

Step 3

Use Self-Talk (Your Own Internal Coach) to Transform Yourself and Reprogram Your Unconscious Mind!

The final step in the A.C.T. Model process involves *talking to yourself,* using that little voice in your head (your own internal coach) to transform yourself to become just like the standard of excellence in your model. You accomplish this by answering these two questions: "How would I have been different if I had been 'excellent' in this performance situation?" "What would have been different *about me* if I had been at the very top of my game, for each descriptor in my personal model of excellence?"

To answer these questions, use imagery associated with your personal standards of excellence and use self-talk to clearly see and feel what and how you would change to embody the ideal standard for each word in your model. Review the situations that occurred over the period you're evaluating and *transform* yourself, using imagery, to respond to those same situations in the way you would like to have responded. In your mind's eye (understanding the difference in "feel" that is associated with such a shift), imagine moving from your actual level of performance (as you perceived it to be) to your ideal level of performance for each of the descriptors in your A.C.T. Model. Imagine yourself transforming from where you were to where you wanted to be. See the metamorphosis involved and imagine what it would feel like to shift to this new mental state. The challenge is to *become* your model of excellence and "live it" in everything you do!

For some individuals, it's very helpful (especially in the early implementation stage of their A.C.T. Model) to build a journal component into their personal logbook. I've built such a component into the logbook that I designed for my clients for many years, and while this type of tool doesn't suit everyone's style, it's been adopted, adapted, and used by many. I include two "self-feedback" forms that have a structure as outlined in Figures 17 and 18.

FIGURE 17: PROBLEM BOX
(where I summarize the problems . . . briefly)

(This form should be **NO BIGGER** than this!)

FIGURE 18: SOLUTIONS BOX
(where I write about solutions; about how I want to be)

(This form should be **MUCH BIGGER** than this!)

With respect to the "Problem Box" shown in Figure 17, it's important to limit the space. The goal of delimiting the size of this area is to force you to encapsulate or summarize the main problem(s) briefly . . . not to spend a lot of time elaborating on the details of the problem. It could be a comment such as: "I didn't do a very good job today at staying focused on the task. I kept letting my mind wander to worry about whether or not I'd be successful." The reason for this decision is simple—Rule #3 of the Rules of the Mental Road informs us that we "Can't NOT think about whatever's on our mind!" The more space we allocate to expand on the negative points that relate to our performance, the more size, weight, color, and structure we give those negative thoughts, entrenching them into our unconscious mind. This isn't an "ostrich with our head in the sand" technique, however. It's important to identify the problem areas we encounter. However, it's sufficient to boil the problem down to its core issues to understand what needs to be changed and how to begin to make that shift.

As far as the "Solutions Box" is concerned (Figure 18), take all the space you want! This is where you would write "notes to self" concerning the correct mindset associated with your ability to perform at an "A" Game level during the performance that you're evaluating. It could be a narrative; it could be bullet point notes—it doesn't matter how you put your thoughts down, but rather that you get them down. Writing them down forces you to consolidate your thoughts concerning the performance that you're self-evaluating to describe the look and feel as well as the actions that you did or would've taken had you performed with excellence. Writing it down also forces you to really focus on what you're doing.

Some clients prefer to create entries associated with each of their A.C.T. Model descriptors while others prefer an overall narrative. There is no correct or incorrect way to accomplish this final step of the process.

By way of example, to describe what kind of information might go into this "Solutions Box," I would like to share with you some actual journal entries taken from the logbook of one of my high-performance clients who visited with me because he was struggling to put together performances at a level that he'd previously delivered with ease. I include this example here only to illustrate how Joe's (this is not his real name) thinking and focus shifted to a more execution-focused mindset as a result of actively engaging his A.C.T. Model, and his logbook entries articulated this change quite well. First, I'll tell you a little about Joe.

Joe was a front tire changer for one of the top NASCAR Cup race teams competing on the circuit that year. He was recognized by many of his peers as being one of the top changers in the business, but of late, he'd been struggling to deliver the kind of pit-stop performance that was essential at this level of competition. The more errors he made, the more he worried about making errors and being slow, and of course, the more he made errors and was indeed slow. As time went on, he worried excessively and focused on the wrong thing. The problem was becoming more serious as he was costing his team as much as 1.5–2 seconds per stop, a huge problem in their world! The team didn't want to let him go, however, because they knew what kind of performance he was capable of, so they asked me to spend some time with him. Together, we developed his A.C.T. Model, and he set to work implementing the process into his racing and his life.

Three of the eight descriptors in Joe's model were "loose," "crisp," and "in control." If you think about what a tire changer must accomplish during a pit stop in a chaotic race situation, these descriptors make sense. The journal entries below are taken verbatim from his personal logbook, purely for the purpose of illustration, from three separate time windows:

- Time 1 (T1): The week after his visit with me when he really had just started working with his personal A.C.T. Model (this coincided with the following weekend race on the competitive calendar).

- Time 2 (T2): Two weeks following Time 1, again at a subsequent race event on the calendar.
- Time 3 (T3): Two weeks following Time 2, at another race.

"LOOSE"

- T1—"Still a little tense from the week before. I would have been a lot better if I didn't have to prove I could do it. A '9' would have been mellow, not so much weight on my shoulders."
- T2—"The loose feeling was great . . . the best I've felt in months. Man, I love that feeling, NO tension. It felt like the weight was lifted off my shoulders."
- T3—"Lighter than anything you could imagine, NO worries, tension, or nervousness. Limber like a piece of thread. Walking tall, head high, shoulders back, feeling really good. Just another walk in the park. Jumping perfectly, landing perfectly, every movement felt looser than ever."

"CRISP"

- T1—"Movements, sight were ok but not up to par. Hand and eye coordination would have been better, more precise. Jabs and pulls would have had less mistakes."
- T2—"Sharp, quick movements felt snappy . . . it felt good. It was like hitting, moving, like you never did before with fun and excitement. It was next to perfect, the way it's supposed to be. The old but new (Joe) is back!"
- T3—"Running to the car, every stride felt solid. Going down on one knee, then the other was firm and precise. Hitting lugs harder than ever, like I was a hydraulic ram. Not rough but sharp, hard, fast jabs. Very stable movements . . . short, sweet, hard, and right on target."

"IN CONTROL"

- T1—"I felt better in control than last week. Need more work in that area. It would have been awesome if I would stop, slow down, and do it. A "9" would have been a mistake free day."
- T2—"I was so focused it felt like nothing could go wrong. Every movement I felt it. The accuracy, the timing of the jump, kneeling down to start, hitting nuts, I was on top of the world . . . unstoppable."
- T3—"So fast, accurate. Movements were precise and on time. I could see a little more detail than usual. So focused the movements felt automatic and natural. I didn't feel rushed or pressured, I was energized. Jumping, running, kneeling, hitting nuts, pulling tires . . . I felt like no energy was used."

Interesting progression of thought over the period of a month, isn't it? Needless to say, as Joe figured out how to control his focus of attention to be on the right things at the right time and was able to direct his thoughts to the specific behaviors and actions that made him the top performer that he was, his performance came back to him. It's indeed funny how that works!

The Holy Grail of the Performance Equation is the ability to focus on the task in front of you, to the exclusion of everything else in that moment that simply serves to distract you from that performance imperative. If you develop the ability to control and sustain that type of focus, you'll deliver the best performances you're capable of. If you help your children to develop this kind of focus as well, this mindset will sustain them as they create moments of virtuosity throughout their lives. It's unreasonable to expect more than that from anyone.

Conclusion

There you have it. The A.C.T. Model is a simple, methodical process of self-analysis and self-correction, but it isn't a magic bullet. It requires deliberate, purposeful, and consistent implementation of a dominant thought control program to change your thinking and your performance. If you apply this process to your work and to your life in general, you *will* become better at getting out of your own way. Your unconscious mind will take its direction from a new set of powerful, positive, and task-focused dominant thoughts, and this mindset will help you to optimize your personal performance. It will also increase the likelihood you'll accomplish the performance goals you set for yourself.

As I stated in the Introduction, my primary goal in writing this book is to indirectly help kids acquire a better understanding of how the way that they think—as they take on the major challenges of their life—affects how they feel, how they behave, and ultimately, how they perform. I realize this is a very tall order indeed, especially since I can't really even get to these kids. But as an important mentor in their life, you can. By helping you to better understand how these basic mental skills factor into the performance equation and by giving you tools to begin to change your own thinking and perspective, I hope to help you become more effective at controlling your own thoughts when your performance is on the line or in the face of life's big challenges. If I am successful at achieving this goal, I'm confident that you'll be more effective at paying it forward with your children.

For many parents, it's difficult to set aside what they want for their children in favor of what the children want for themselves. It's also sometimes hard for parents to accept that not all children are athletically or artistically inclined. This doesn't mean that they can't enjoy and benefit from participation in sport activities or the performance arts, but rather that they may not possess the body type, the talent, or the desire to excel in these activities or even to pursue this type of involvement at a high level.

A child's developmental needs can often be best served by exposing them to as many different activities (sports, music, the performance arts, etc.) as possible at a young age to provide them with a variety of experiences. This will give them an idea of what's out there and what's available to them until they get a clearer picture of what they're passionate about. Generally, with a good foundation of active participation in a variety of sports and other activities, there will be plenty of time to streamline them into the particular activity they may wish to pursue more seriously, once they've sampled the broad "menu" of offerings and determined what that might be.

Each of us has the choice to think and act either positively or negatively, constructively or destructively. Given this basic truth, why on earth would anyone purposefully set about thinking negatively? We don't deliberately choose to think this way and our children don't either. The point is that we don't *consciously* make a choice each time we think. Our unconscious mind predisposes us to one type of thinking or another, based upon our personal mental programming—which is based upon our overriding dominant thought. Old thought patterns *can* be replaced with new, more productive mental programs; it just takes the will to do so and the consistent work necessary to achieve it. It involves increasing your level of awareness of what you want to change and consciously repeating the new program you desire over and over again in your imagination. That's what the A.C.T. Model process is designed to do.

How will you know that your A.C.T. Model is working? How does it express itself in the things you do? There are as many different applications of this performance-modeling process as there are individuals and situations that they find themselves in. Let me offer a simple example that may help you to understand how the process can be integrated into any task that someone might undertake and how it has the potential to change their actual performance.

Let's imagine that the person in question is getting ready to head into an important meeting where they must present their analysis of a complex work situation and outline specific recommendations for action. If they're successful at making their case, the company will move in a particular direction, but if they're not, management may decide to head in a different direction. There's a lot of money at stake, and it's a pressure-filled situation because there are competing solutions being considered.

For some individuals who are thrust into this type of situation, their overriding response as they step into the meeting room is one of worry. They dwell on the fact that if they're unsuccessful in convincing the company's executive team about the benefits of their solution over that of other strategies being considered, the company may make a mistake as far as they're concerned and lose a lot of money. In addition, they may worry that failure to make their case might undermine the confidence they believe senior management has had in their decision-making ability in the past. Perhaps they beat themselves up over prior mistakes and the less-than-ideal results they may have realized in similar situations in the past and fear that a similar outcome may come to pass this time as well.

This "fear of failure" becomes dominant in their conscious mind, and this thought process causes their anxiety to increase. This anxiety leads to tunnel vision, and they lose the mental flexibility needed to think clearly on their feet. As they worry more and more that their fears may be realized, they look to their audience for signs to confirm their fears. They mentally talk themselves into the very thing they fear the most. They end up focusing less on the content and the connection they're making with their audience and more on the thought that they're not getting the job done. Failure threatens even more to become a self-fulfilling prophecy.

With an A.C.T. Model to guide their thinking, however, the situation could be different. The meeting is just as important, and the situation offers just as much pressure as it did before, but their personal response to it is different. As they begin to engage their personal model of excellence in advance of the meeting, they remind themselves that they can't control the outcome of the meeting. They take the time to understand that the outcome they're working toward has a greater chance of being realized if they remain calm, confident, and task-focused. As they prepare for their meeting, they recall past experiences where they have been successful and gradually come to adopt the same mindset they possessed when they did well in similar situations in the past. As they step through the descriptors of their personal A.C.T. Model in their conscious mind—descriptors that define who they are and how they think when they do their best work—their unconscious mind responds and takes them to that place.

They enter the meeting room with a more task-focused and calm mindset, and since this mindset influences their thinking in the moment, they don't become preoccupied by negative thoughts associated with anxiety and failure. They're more likely to connect with their audience and clearly outline their ideas and plan in the most effective way possible. Because they're more relaxed and tuned in to the issues and concerns that are of specific interest to individual executive team members, they respond more effectively to any questions that are raised. All things being equal, what situation do you believe is likely to yield the better result?

The vast majority of high-performance people would agree that 80% of the performance game is mental. They recognize that it's not their physical prowess or their knowledge that ensures success in the competitive world in which they live and work. Rather, they realize that their personal success is most influenced by the mental skills they're able to bring to bear on the tasks they undertake on a day-to-day basis and at the very moment of the major events in their lives.

Even though mental skills are acknowledged as being a critically important part of the Performance Equation, most of us invest little time and effort in working on this aspect of our personal performance. Part of the reason stems from the trait characteristic that we human beings possess that causes us to look for the easy way to do just about everything. The marketplace is filled with financially successful products that promise the "quick fix," the modern-day equivalent of the "magic pill." But developing mental toughness is not unlike developing physical fitness. It takes time, effort, and dedication to develop the kind of mental toughness that high-performance people work diligently to develop.

As you improve your mental skills, you'll learn to associate the images and feelings of what you're like (what it "feels" like) when you're appropriately focused and on task. Once you're aware of these images and feelings, you'll be able to more effectively apply this improved control over your focus of attention to other complex tasks you might undertake. You must provide your unconscious mind with a new goal image if you want to bring about change; otherwise, it will automatically refer back to previous programming for its instructions. You always act the part, unconsciously, of the person you see yourself to be. It's important to choose wisely.

With quality practice, you'll understand how to control and direct your focus so that it's appropriate to the demands of any activity in which you're involved. If you successfully integrate the seven key Rules of the Mental Road into your day-to-day thinking (and maintain that mindset—*this is the key*), you will possess the secret of how to program your mind for success. You'll understand how to shape your dominant thought so that you can more easily slip into your mental zone of peak performance on command.

Remember that your mind can only actively process one thought at a time (Rule #2), and the truth is that you can't NOT think about whatever's on your mind (Rule #3). As a result, your performance will be best served by implanting a dominant program in your mind that describes exactly what you want and how you want to be when you perform at your best *in the moment.* If you focus on this mental program, you'll find it easier to maintain the relaxed and confident frame of mind that's consistent with your best personal performance.

Ultimately, it's about control, and this is the kind of control we would want our children to have. Control over their thoughts so that they consciously adopt the best possible perspective in the face of any challenge that life throws in their way and, when it comes time for them to perform, to be able to do so, being fully present as they focus on the task at hand.

What can you control? You can control your thinking if you take the time to become aware of it and take command of it. You can control the things you choose to believe and the way you see yourself (your perspective). You can control what you imagine and the direction in which you want your future to unfold. You can control the goals you set for yourself and the way you go about achieving them. You can control the things you eat and the exercise you engage in. You can control with whom you associate and the topics of conversation you're willing to engage in. You can control the environment you learn and live in, and the people, places, and things that influence your thinking and behavior. You can control *your response* to every situation and circumstance in your life. It's a fact that *the human mind doesn't distinguish between what's real and what's vividly imagined!* This basic truth applies to every single role and aspect of your life. It's not just about your work or about the competitive environment; these principles are fundamental, universal, and infallible . . . and they apply to every aspect and role in your life.

The A.C.T. Model process is a tool you can use to help you to get the most out of yourself in everything that you do. As you come to understand its founding principles more clearly, you can also help your children, over time by your example and coaching, to develop a Performance Thinking mindset that will sustain them for the rest of their lives. As I mentioned at the start of this book, children don't come with an instruction manual, and we don't know what we don't know until we know it. I hope this book has helped you to understand the mental-skills part of the performance game a little better. In closing, I encourage you to remember this basic truth as you forge ahead on your journey:

In the moment of your performance, it's impossible to do better than the best you can do. So just focus on what you can control and work diligently to bring the best that you've got to whatever it is you're engaged in!

Be well, and good luck!

Jacques Dallaire, Ph.D.

About the Author

Jacques Dallaire, Ph.D., received his doctorate in Exercise Physiology from the University of Alberta (Canada) in 1979. He taught at McGill University in Montreal for five years before assuming the then-newly created position of Manager of Science and Medicine Programs at Sport Canada (a division of the Canadian Government's Ministry of Fitness and Amateur Sport). While at Sport Canada, Dr. Dallaire was responsible for the management of the Sport Science Support Program, which provided funding to more than forty national sport governing bodies, to support their sport science initiatives. He was also on the review panel for the Sport Science Research Program and served as the liaison between the government of Canada and the Sports Medicine Council of Canada and its four professional member organizations.

Dr. Dallaire relocated to the Untied States in 1992 to develop a comprehensive performance-enhancement program under the name Human Performance International, where he served as president for eight years. In 1998, he moved to the Charlotte, NC area where he ultimately formed Performance Prime and currently serves as its president.

Over the past forty years, Dr. Dallaire has worked directly with thousands of individuals from the high-performance sport world and beyond, including law enforcement, the entertainment world, and the business community. Dr. Dallaire divides his time between delivering sports team and corporate group performance programs as well as individual, one-on-one programs with high-performance competitors. He is a founding member of the International Council of Motorsport Sciences, a board member of the Stand 21 "Racing Goes Safer" Foundation, and in 2007, he was inducted into the Canadian Motorsports Hall of Fame in recognition of his innovative, state-of-the-art training strategies and the impact he has had on the sport.

Made in the USA
Middletown, DE
21 December 2017